The CBT Workbook for Anxiety

Rewire Your Mind With Cognitive
Behavioral Therapy Techniques to
Promote a Positive Mindset and
Overcome Depression

Shirley R. Lynn

TABLE OF CONTENTS

INTRODUCTION

● ● ● ● ● ● ● ● ● ● ● ● ● ● ●

Sara sits in front of me, her hands unconsciously twisting the floral print skirt she is wearing. Her eyes are red-rimmed, and I can see she has recently been crying. She is trying so bravely to appear normal and okay.

"Sara," I say, "You're in a safe place here. Let's start with what's going on for you right now." As she pours out a long list of complaints and frustrations about her work, her kids, her workload at home and her mother, the same picture builds that I see with most of my anxious clients. Well, not exactly the same; the colors and shapes might be slightly different, but the frame is overfull with complexity. And it is not a pretty picture.

Sara is not unique in that way. Our complex lives mean that anxiety disorders are one of the most common problems we face these days. About 4% of the world's population suffers from anxiety, to the point that it is seriously disruptive in their lives. That's around 275 million people to put it in perspective (Fleming, 2019).

Anxiety is not just a bad feeling. Our minds affect our bodies, and vice versa, so the results of untreated, ongoing anxiety can include IBS (Irritable Bowel Syndrome) and other digestive upset and stomach pain, high blood pressure, angina, panic attacks, headaches, irritability in general, depression, loss of libido, extreme fatigue and all kinds of aches and pains. It has even been cited as a trigger for arthritis and other chronic problems (PatientPop Inc, 2021).

It is not something someone is 'putting on', 'playing up', doing to 'seek attention', or a choice people deliberately make. It needs to be taken seriously. Believe me, if you have ever battled anxiety, you will know you would do anything not to feel that way.

If you suffer from anxiety, then you will know the feeling Sara is sharing with me. Your heart is pounding. It feels like a giant hand is squeezing your insides so you can barely breathe. Every cell in your body is buzzing like a crazed electric circuit gone wrong, your stomach is tying itself in complicated and unexpected knots, and, if you could, you would disappear.

Except there is nowhere to go where you won't feel like this. And the frustrating thing is that right now there is no clear reason you can see for this feeling. It just arrives at the strangest times: sometimes when you are at the mall, sometimes on that self-care walk on the beach, and often in the middle of the night. It's an extremely unwelcome guest, like a pesky neighbour who drops in for tea without warning and at the worst times, leaving you exhausted and annoyed.

Somewhere along the line, anxiety creeps in and makes itself at home, and this is a houseguest you could really do without. How do you get it to leave? "Just relax," some say, "It's not that bad. You'll be fine!" They must be the lucky ones who have never truly felt like this. Or won't admit it, if they have.

You've tried the self-care bit. But bubble baths, naps and chocolates don't cut it. Not much seems to keep this feeling away for long, and you feel stuck, perhaps even hopeless. Medication works, if you can afford it, but who wants to stay medicated 24/7 for the rest of their lives?

As a coach and therapist, I see this almost every day. People strung out, stressed out, lost, confused, and unable to process these feelings. They don't even know where to start, and it is a crying shame because it seems we are taught so much about keeping our bodies healthy, about how to treat physical wounds, and next to nothing about how to keep our minds and hearts healthy too.

As I support each client through this healing journey, the comments are almost always the same: "Once you know it, it is so simple." This statement is not meant to minimize the problem, but the solutions to feeling better, and to being more in control of your inner world, are not complicated. You don't have to sit in a lotus position for five hours humming mantras, or travel to Tibet, for the answers.

I have the answers for you right here, in this book you've decided to pick up today. While some of the methods and tools mentioned here will create a feeling of ease almost immediately, healing the brain, and undoing the learning and patterns that led to your anxiety, may take a bit longer. It varies from person to person, but each small shift you make will add up until eventually life starts feeling a whole lot easier and better. There is no one quick fix, but, instead, many little approaches that I will ask you to think about and try. Each one builds on the others until you have a toolbox of actions you can take that will altogether make you a stronger, more resilient person.

I can personally attest to most of these methods, as I have used them myself during a particularly low period in my life when a bad relationship pushed me to my limits. Even though I already had a Bachelor's degree in Social Relations from Radcliffe College and my Ph.D. in Psychology from Cornell University, that didn't mean I had all the answers yet or knew how to consistently apply them in my own life. Knowing is different from doing. This was a time that challenged me so much that anxiety became an everyday companion to me. That was when I realized that mental and emotional hygiene need to be an everyday practice for all of us, and that we need easy-to-use tools that are easier to access than waiting for the next talk therapy session.

Not that I want to put therapists and life coaches out of business. After all, I am one myself. But these anxiety-management skills need to be common household knowledge. Your external support systems, like therapists, coaches and counsellors, can provide guidance to you on a more advanced level, whereas the suggestions in this book are techniques you can use everyday if you choose to.

Once you have worked through the practical and easy-to-use content in this super-chill workbook, you will find that the next time anxiety wants to pay you a visit, you are not at home for it.

It's time to take back control of your life, and it is totally possible to feel better, consistently. Cognitive Behavioral Therapy (CBT) is a commonly used approach that works extremely well, getting to the root of your thoughts and feelings and helping you to create more supportive and constructive behavior patterns.

Using a holistic combination of CBT, as well as a few other tools and practices I have found effective for managing anxiety, you will be able to apply these skills in your own life, and even share them with friends and family to spread your newfound happiness and calm around.

Or maybe you are a life coach or counsellor yourself, in which case the exercises here are all easily printable for you to use in your own practice. I believe in sharing these tools freely because the more people who have access to them, the better and less anxious a place the world will be. It is my ultimate hope that one day these things will be taught to every child at school, and the cycle of pain, stress, and anxiety we are currently witnessing in our society will be broken before it even starts.

Take the time, read the supporting information, do the exercises, and maybe even redo them as your understanding spirals higher so that you can come back to familiar concepts at a more advanced level. It is time to feel better, and it is within your power to do so if you put the effort in. Most of these tools do not require a whole lot of effort either. I understand when you are feeling low, that most things can feel too much, so I have made these pages as simple to follow as possible. These are tools I use, that most of my clients use, and that many of my associates have also shared in the past. Put simply: they work.

Now, let's begin this healing journey together.

CHAPTER 1:
THE ANXIOUS BRAIN

E ven though we have neuroscience and MRI (Magnetic Resonance Imaging) scans that can tell us a lot about the brain these days, there are still big gaps in the understanding of what creates an anxiety disorder.

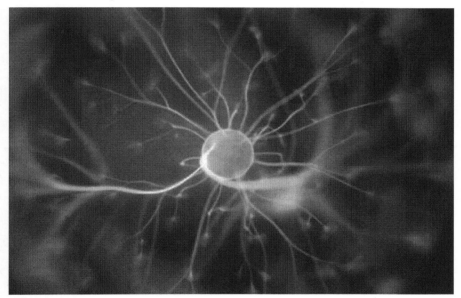

Let's try and break it down a bit.

BRAIN EVOLUTION AND SURVIVAL TACTICS

Scientists have isolated certain parts of the brain with relation to anxiety: the amygdala, which processes emotions and instincts; the hippocampus, which processes short into long-term memory; the hypothalamus, which controls energy levels (like the extra sugars you need when fighting or running); and the prefrontal cortex, which regulates impulses and emotions (Smith, n.d). These same areas of the brain suffer the most when we are exposed to constant, unmanaged stress.

Fear, which is a natural survival response, is present for most people; we need it to survive. Fear keeps us from stepping into a busy road, off a cliff, or petting that tiger at the zoo. But, we need to learn to manage fear, or it will manage us.

Our brains have evolved over many millennia, and archeologists and other researchers have shown that, from the so-called 'caveman days' to now, our brains really haven't changed that much (Robson, 2011). Back in those days a certain set of responses were required to survive in harsh eat-or-be-eaten conditions. Our brains and bodies colluded to set up a great system to help us react fast to danger: this is the well-known fight-flight-freeze response. When we perceive that there is potential danger nearby, our brain sends signals to our body and releases a variety of chemicals, like adrenaline and cortisol, that all help us move faster, be stronger, feel less pain, and so on, so that we can either run like the wind away from the perceived danger, or fight off the huge ravenous beasts, other cavemen, or whatever it is that wants to hurt us. The freeze function lets us sit very, very still, so that danger hopefully passes by without even seeing us.

Fast forward about 30 000 years, and we live in a very different environment. Now what is dangerous and what is not is less clear, and our poor brains tend to react to all perceived threats and don't seem to be able to effectively distinguish between real danger and misguided perceptions of danger. These are many, from the boss in a bad mood, to the busy traffic, to a spam call, a piece of news about a disaster anywhere in the world, or the sound of a siren in the distance. Our brains end up being on almost permanent alert, and that can only lead to feeling hypervigilant and anxious a lot of the time.

Heightened anxiety can be environmental, as we have just described, but we can also be more genetically predisposed to it. Some people have brain synapses (the receptors on each neuron) that have mutated to resist proper absorption of serotonin (one of our feel-good chemicals that counters stress) and need help with increasing this absorption process between neurons. Serotonin Reuptake Inhibitors (SRIs) are antidepressant medications that help stop our neurons from repelling serotonin so that we can use it optimally (asapscience, 2017).

Anything that inflames the brain can also aggravate anxiety responses. Inflammation can result from a poor diet or from existing inflammation in the body due to infections, gut problems, or autoimmune conditions (Schmee, 2021). Caffeine, nicotine, and alcohol are some of the common things we use that can also heighten anxiety systems via our brain-body connection. They mimic the effects of stress, such as increased heart rate, and so give us a reverse anxiety in that because our body is behaving this way we may assume we are feeling anxious even when there is no other trigger.

Moreover, a very traumatic event, at any time in our lives, can be severe enough that it primes us to be more vigilant and reactive than normal to any future perceived problems. I say perceived because a lot of what goes on in our lives is not based on real or immediate danger, such as something we need to actually fight off or flee from. Our angry boss will not kill us, hopefully,and running away every time they walk into the office may be a little awkward. That siren is nowhere near our work or our home, but we still react to it.

If we are reminded of a past trauma, our amygdala lights up, acting just the same as if the traumatic event was happening again. Our prefrontal cortex becomes sluggish as our fight-or-flight response kicks in; this means that we become less able to control the fear, a reaction that sits at the root of what we call PTSD (Post-traumatic Stress Disorder).

As you can see there are many possible neurological reasons why we may feel anxious. Regardless of the root cause, the ultimate effect is pretty much the same: in most cases, even though our bodies are flooded with survival chemicals, the actual situation does not call for us to fight, run, or hide. Thus, the chemicals don't get used up in these activities, and they remain in our systems for hours, pumping us full of extra sugars (energy), heightening our senses, raising our heart rates and generally making us feel anxious and stressed out.

Some people even seek out this adrenaline rush by putting themselves into 'controlled' danger, like skydiving, ziplining, watching horror movies, bungee jumping, and so on. And yes, watching horror movies counts, as the subconscious can't differentiate between real and unreal so we still get a fright even though we logically know we are safe sitting on our couch in the lounge.

But, because most of us aren't taught what to do about the situation, we find ourselves, over time, dealing with the effects of having these chemicals in our systems way more than we actually need them. Consequently, over time, we get hardwired for stress and become ever more reactive and sensitive to external triggers of all kinds. Our blood vessels and heart experience extra wear and tear, our risk of heart attack or stroke goes up, we put on weight, become insomniacs and become hypervigilant and irritable. Anxiety, at this point, becomes a common part of our lives, and one we could most certainly do without. We become more likely to become its victim, simply because we do not understand how to manage our fearful thoughts, or process the fear chemicals in our bodies.

CBT helps with this situation by reframing thoughts, which in turn help reprogramme these fight-or-flight reactions and lessen the severity of the impact they have on our lives. A holistic view to processing stress chemicals is also very useful, and we will cover that in the next chapter.

PRACTICAL EXERCISE: IS ANXIETY A PROBLEM FOR ME?

A minor level of anxiety now and then is quite normal. Feeling anxious before an exam, or in a job interview is understandable. However, feeling anxious more often than not, and in unexpected, non-pressurized situations, might be an indication that it is time to get help.

Rate yourself against the following statements, with 'never', 'seldom', 'sometimes', or 'all the time' as your options.

How often do you feel...	Never	Seldom (once or twice a month)	Sometimes (every week)	All the time (every day)
Stressed				
Frustrated				
Pressurized				
Confused				
Worried				
Disconnected				
Overwhelmed				
Angry/Irritable				
Restless				
Fearful				

If you answered 'sometimes' or 'all the time' to any of these, this is a red flag that anxiety management may be an issue in your life that needs some attention.

Anxiety symptoms may show up as any combination of the following:

1. Increased heart beat, trembling, shaking, sweating
2. Clenched muscles, hands and jaw

3. Stomachache or a general feeling of discomfort and being unwell or nauseous
4. Aching muscles and jaw (from all the clenching)
5. Higher-pitched voice, due to vocal chords constricting
6. Heavier than normal breathing
7. A tight feeling in your chest
8. Restlessness
9. Obsessive and/or racing thoughts
10. Random bursts of irritability
11. Nitpicking and trying to make things perfect
12. Pacing or zoning out

A regular or healthy amount of anxiety would include things like worrying about money, exams or big events, the reaction and grief right after losing a loved one, or fear of real dangers, like a large, barking dog off its leash. You still want to get a handle on this before it becomes more serious, but the frequency is less severe and worrisome.

An anxiety disorder involves:

1. Difficulty completing everyday tasks due to constant worry
2. Irrational fears of normally non-threatening situations, like talking to people, taking an elevator, or driving to the shop

3. Continual flashbacks to past trauma, triggering a whole trauma response each time

4. Obsessive behavior to help self-soothe, like cleaning, rearranging, checking stuff over and over again in a short period of time

5. Panic attacks, and the fear of having another panic attack, which can often bring on an actual panic attack

If any of the above resonates with you, I would strongly recommend getting external help as well as working through this book. Often it has taken us years to develop a full-blown anxiety disorder, and it will take time, patience, support and understanding to heal it and learn to manage it.

TYPES OF FEAR

Before we become anxious there is generally a mental thought trigger (unless we have a direct physical reason at the root, like brain inflammation or a chemical imbalance).

As we have mentioned, fear is a necessary element of our existence. Within reason it keeps us safe. We can't get rid of fear, but we can learn to manage it better. To do so we need to understand it more.

Rational fears are the ones we need to leave as is. They are our response to real danger. If you have a near collision in traffic or your kid is about to put their finger in an open plug socket, a fear response helps you act quickly to avoid danger and your actions help use up the stress chemicals released in your body.

Irrational fear is your body responding to a stimulus that is not an immediate, clear, and present danger. These fears are what we target with CBT to help reduce and manage them. Some common irrational fears include:

1. Fear of exclusion, loss of respect, criticism or rejection. Being judged unworthy, shoved out of the group, and left alone, where we are more vulnerable. While in the old days being evicted from the tribe could certainly mean death, now if we

are disapproved of or excluded, it is not so life-threatening. But it can still feel that it is, on an instinctual level.

This type of fear can also start from a young age and be exacerbated by very demanding caregivers who link us meeting their desires to a conditional love. For example, "Do this, say this, or be this, and then I will love you." The child links safety to getting things right and pleasing those in power. Another root cause of this is when we don't get our most basic needs met as infants, and develop an insecure attachment style. This continues into adulthood on a subconscious level and can lead to people pleasing, a need to be perfect, and anxiety if we feel the least bit left out or unwanted.

2. Fear that you don't know enough. We have a very fault-finding, marks-based, get-it-right-or-else mindset that starts in school and can dog us all of our days if we let it. It can lead to a need for perfectionism that limits our growth because we are too scared to make mistakes, which also means we are afraid to try anything new. We need to allow ourselves to make mistakes in order to learn. As young children, we don't let perfectionism stop us from trying to walk. If that was the case, none of us would do it. But as we get older and our ego steps in more, we start doubting and second-guessing ourselves.

   Fear of failure is a branch of this category. If you don't ever try, you think you can't fail, but instead you fail by default because nothing happens. Procrastinators often get stuck because of this fear.

3. Fear of success or change. If we change something about ourselves it might wreck what is working now. Or we think that, since we are comfortable as we are, why fix something that is not broken. The reality is that the world never stops changing, and we need to be okay with continually pushing just a little outside our comfort zones in order to adapt along with it. If we don't, eventually external changes will lead to some sort of breakdown in the smooth running of our lives, and we will then be forced to make drastic changes whether we like it or not.

The irony is that comfort zones slowly become less comfortable over time, anyway. You know you are in need of change if you are feeling lacklustre, bored, unmotivated, tired, irritable, and uninspired by life.

4. Fear of ill health, disability, old age, or death. On one side of the spectrum this is a rational fear that keeps us safe, but on the other it could limit our lives if taken too far.

5. Fear of not having enough. This is normally linked to money, but can also be linked to resources in general. This can keep us in jobs, relationships, behavior patterns, or lifestyles that don't make us happy. Fearing hardship and poverty is not entirely irrational, and yet, if it keeps you stuck in a rut, it is also unhealthy.

We are only born with two fears: a fear of falling and a fear of loud noises (James, 2020). The rest develop over time as we grow and experience life, and as we are taught how to be in the world by others.

PRACTICAL EXERCISE: IDENTIFYING MY FEARS

Let's take a look at what might be triggering you to experience your specific fears. You can either do this retrospectively, if you have a good memory, or carry a small notebook around for a week or so. Either way, make a note of the following:

1. Try to remember or identify times when you have felt nervous or scared. This includes waking in the night with specific fears, nightmares, etc.
2. What happened directly before that (series of events or context)?
3. What were you thinking at the time, especially right before the feeling?
4. Are there any areas of your life you try to keep tight control of or avoid? We often try to control or avoid certain situations to reduce fears.
5. What makes you angry? Sometimes fear lies underneath anger, so if so, what fear is lurking behind your anger?

6. Is there an area of your life you really want to change, but never get around to doing anything about? This may be an indication of fear of failure or change.
7. What behavior usually follows these bad feelings?
8. Can you see a pattern to the events or thoughts?
9. What do you think are your top five fears or worries?
10. Are these fears real (ie: if they happened they could cause serious harm to you or others), or are they not so real or harmful?
11. What can you do more, or less, to make things calmer for yourself?

Don't worry about worrying; If a fear can be learned, it can be unlearned too.

To take this exercise to the next level, you can jump ahead to Chapter Six and do the fear and risk exercises there too. Just don't forget to jump back here and carry on afterwards.

THE SYMPATHETIC AND PARASYMPATHETIC NERVOUS SYSTEM

Our autonomic (that is, happens automatically without conscious effort) nervous system has two categories: sympathetic, which is the fight-flight response mentioned earlier, and parasympathetic, which is the opposite. The parasympathetic response is activated when our bodies and minds rest, and energy is re-established to things like digestion, eating, making more humans, and so on. These are all things that are safe to do when there is no danger.

But, as we know, there are many situations that can throw these two systems out of balance, leaving you more in the high-energy, ready-for-danger state that is not good for anyone long term.

Sympathetic System	Parasympathetic System
The fight, flight, or freeze response.	The rest and digest response.
Prepares you for any potential danger.	Brings you to a state of calm.
The sympathetic system has shorter neuron pathways, and thus a quicker response time.	Has longer neuron pathways, and thus a slower response time.
Heartbeat increases, muscles tense.	Heartbeat decreases, muscles relax.
Pupils dilate to let in more light so you can see better.	Pupils contract back to normal.
Saliva secretion decreases and digestion slows.	Saliva secretion and digestion resume.
Adrenaline is released and extra glycogen is converted to glucose (energy).	No adrenaline released. System and sugar remain stable.

While the autonomic nervous system is mainly not a conscious process we can totally control, we can learn some tips and tricks to keep it more on the rest and digest side and less in the alert state. Ultimately, our brains are not at fault; they are merely survival mechanisms programmed to keep us safe. But, luckily, we have a few factors in our favor: We are able to shift and change our triggering thoughts, we can reframe and reprogramme how we respond to external stressors, and we have a wonderfully neuroplastic brain. New brain cells and connections are forming all the time, and we can choose to do certain things that will encourage this brain hardware's healing process.

CHAPTER 2:
THE ANXIOUS BODY

* * * * * * * * * * * * *

We have all heard that old maxim that the brain and body are linked. But, as we go about our daily lives, we often feel like we are a separate entity to our physical forms. Sometimes we place our sense of self in our heads, where the brain sits, and reign from there like some autocratic overlord, commanding the rest of our self to just fall in line. You probably know what happened sometime between the middle ages and now: The autocratic overlords got overthrown by the hardworking lower classes, who, as it turned out, were every bit as important to a functioning society as the glamorous dudes in cloth-of-gold on smart horses.

But enough stories; the science is in, too: The brain is connected to the rest of the body via neural pathways that both signal the rest of the body, and receive signals from the body. The gut contains neurons, and the vagus nerve between gut and brain also regulates digestion,

heart rate, breathing, some reflexes and blood vessel dilation and constriction. Sensory organs carry messages to the brain, triggering memories, thoughts and certain responses, like fight-or-flight.

If any part of this entire system goes down, it all goes haywire. An inflamed gut affects immune responses, brain function, allergies, absorption (or not) of vital nutrients needed for healthy overall functioning. An inflamed brain affects everything negatively, and causes negative moods like anxiety and depression. The wrong diet, or dehydration or fever in the body, inflames the brain. And round and round it all goes. We need to slowly introduce some calm and restore order to this system.

GET THE BASICS RIGHT

We are so quick to jump to conclusions around our physical and mental health. We may label ourselves, or get a medical diagnosis and expensive medications, before we have considered if we are giving our bodies the basic items needed to operate efficiently.

This sort of check-in should always be your first port of call. Especially as we now know how the body and mind connect, when we aren't feeling our best emotionally, we need to check that our bodies are okay before we assume that there might be some deeper, more sinister problem afoot.

Just like a parent learns with a small child to check all the basics first, so we need to do this with ourselves. When we are tired, ill, in pain, hungry, thirsty, or uncomfortable, we tend to have much less tolerance for any challenges life sends our way. If we are depriving our brain and body of vital nutrients, or giving them too many of the wrong ones, we make it incredibly hard to stay calm, peaceful and happy. An inflamed, malfunctioning body or brain spells disaster and can sit at the root of our anxiety.

We need to make sure we are doing the physical self-care needed to provide all the building blocks for physical and mental health.

DIET

Our modern-day diets, stuffed with additives, preservatives, highly processed foods, and those high in sugars and fats and low in nutritious goodness, are terrible for weight and mood management. Our systems are designed for a simpler time when we were hunter-gatherers and had a wide variety of plants as the main part of our diets. This we added to with whatever small animals, eggs, fish, nuts, seeds, grains, legumes, and even insects, we could find. Sometimes we were lucky and the hunters brought back bigger game to eat, but this was not an everyday occurrence. This is the environmental context our bodies understand and are set up to deal with.

Then along came mass production and biochemical science, and suddenly in this last century or so we have bombarded our poor, confused systems with a lot of stuff we are simply not set up to digest. This creates a chemical storm of confusion in our bodies and leads to all kinds of lifestyle issues, such as inflammation, arthritis, diabetes, weight problems, heart and blood pressure complications and more. Add to that substances like caffeine, alcohol and other stimulants that drive our heart rate up artificially, and we have an even better breeding ground for feelings of anxiety.

How can you drink six or seven cups of strong coffee plus sugar every day, or multiple cans of sugary soda, or energy drinks, and be surprised when your heart is pounding and you can't sleep? It should be a no-brainer, and yet many of us have done something similar on a regular basis.

In general, the following is a good guideline for improving both health and mood:

1. Go for a wide variety of food types and colors. Choose from whole grains, legumes, fruits, nuts, seeds, vegetables, lean proteins, dairy, eggs, fish and seafood.
2. Choose unprocessed, prepared and cooked-from-scratch food whenever you can. If that's not possible, there are many food

outlets and meal production and delivery services that now cater for the health conscious. You can even plan, prepare and freeze meals ahead. Freezing locks in nutritional goodness and it is easy to defrost a ready-made, homemade meal if you don't have time to cook from scratch every day.

3. Cut back on added fats, sugars and all the additives you naturally find in processed food to improve shelf life, color, taste and texture. Reduce the sugar you add to your hot drinks, and consider replacing it with a healthy sweetener like xylitol if you must. Over time you will find that your taste buds wake up and heal from the shock of all the oversweet flavors, and you start enjoying the natural sweetness in your fruits and other foods more. For a sweet treat try berries, frozen/mashed banana, dark chocolate (in moderation), date balls, peanut butter with dark chocolate chips and so on. There are loads of sugar-free options in the diabetic section of supermarkets and stacks of recipes and ideas online.

4. Avoid energy bars, drinks, and sugary sodas. Many of these are loaded with caffeine and other stimulants that may give you a temporary perk, but weaken your entire system in the long run.

5. If you must have caffeine, try it sugar free, watch the amount and stop drinking it well before bedtime.

6. Choose water or herbal teas over other drinks. You can make it more exciting by drinking soda water, and adding a squeeze of fresh orange or lemon to the mix. Berries, and cucumbers are great left to infuse in a jug of cool water. Or add your own favorite mix of fruit slices for extra zing.

7. Keep hydrated. The average recommendation is around eight glasses of water per day, but if your mouth feels dry this means that you are already quite dehydrated. This can affect sugar levels, not to mention pretty much all of your body's vital processes and needs, and make you feel pretty rotten. Carrying bottled water around with you during the day is one way to ensure you drink enough.

8. Consider supplementing your diet with 'good mood foods' like blueberries, bananas, fatty fish, dark chocolate, oats, nuts and seeds.

9. Natural, herbal and nutritional supplements can also help with anxiety levels. Valerian, chamomile and l-theanine are all over-the-counter options to help keep calm. Upping your levels of omega 3 is also beneficial. Go for a supplement with high EPA (Eicosapentaenoic Acid) and DHA (Docosahexaenoic Acid) levels for greater systemic support.

10. Be mindful of your gut health. Include fermented foods like kefir, unsweetened/plain yogurt, tempeh, miso, kimchi and sauerkraut in your diet where you can, and consider supplementing with a probiotic to support gut health. This in turn reduces overall inflammation, allergies, digestive issues and increases absorption of nutrients in general, therefore contributing to a happier brain.

Eat with health as your top priority, and consider each bite in terms of its health value before putting it in your mouth. Of course you will still want a slice of cake or a biscuit from time to time, but if you are on average making healthier choices then your body won't be impacted so badly by the occasional treat.

ACTIVITY LEVELS

Not everyone is a fan of exercise. If you love it and already do it regularly, good job. For the rest of us, we need to find some way to increase our physical movement that makes sense for us, and that we can somehow enjoy.

Although many people think exercise is all about losing weight, in fact that's about the last thing it does for you. It takes about an hour of brisk activity to lose the calorie equivalent of an eclair, so that's just not the optimal approach to concerns about weight.

This is one of the first things I check with my clients, simply because a little bit of activity can mean a huge improvement in mood. Of course, exercise also tones and strengthens muscles, improves overall endurance and fitness and helps you sleep better. But, for me, the main goal is to help people manage their overwhelming feelings.

Physical activity is directly linked to increased serotonin levels (the feel-good brain chemical that you want more of), and also stimulates neurogenesis which helps the brain heal and grow extra connections. It also increases endorphin (more feel-good chemicals) levels, and takes your focus off your troubles for a little while. This is all good stuff!

Studies have shown that exercise is as effective as antidepressants in many cases, and with fewer side effects (Netz, 2017). On average, all you need is around half an hour of exercise, three to four times a week, to make a difference to your mood. You can start out with a few minutes every other day and slowly increase it as you feel able. Also remember to choose an activity you are likely to do, whether that's dancing in your lounge to your favorite tunes, or walking around the block at work, or some simple, quick calisthenics while watching a TV program.

SLEEP

If you are always feeling tired, pretty much everything else feels impossible. Sleep deprivation is a prime breeding ground for frustration, conflict and heightened anxiety.

Sleep is so important for mood management. While you sleep, your brain has the chance to detox and get rid of any buildup of waste materials from the day's activities. It also regenerates and grows new neurons and sorts through all the input (thoughts, feelings, experiences) of the day. In a sense, it filters out what is seen as unhelpful and moves more significant memories into long-term storage, literally cleaning up the 'hard-drive' to get it ready for the next day. Also, sleep allows the rest of your body time to recuperate and replenish itself.

If you are watching both your diet and activity levels, it will contribute towards better sleep. There are also many other things you need to add to that to make sleep easier and better for you. Again, there are a multitude of building blocks, and all are needed to build a quality sleep experience.

1. Try to get some exposure to sunshine (natural light) during the day, consider blue light filters for your devices, and get off all screens well before bedtime. Your brain signals your body to

produce sleep chemicals based on light and activity levels, so as the day winds down, reduce light and any pursuit that is too exciting. Quiet reading, journaling, meditation, and even some light yoga stretches are more advisable than sitting watching a busy TV program or working on your administrative tasks last thing before bed.

2. Make sure your sleep context is supportive. This means that you need to be comfortable enough to fall, and stay, asleep. There should be as little light as possible; blockout curtains are a great way to achieve this. Sounds need to be muffled, absent, or masked with white noise (which you can find on apps and Youtube if you need to). Bedding and pillows need to be soft and comfy, as must the clothing you choose to sleep in. Lastly, the temperature of the room ideally needs to be around 18 degrees celsius.

3. Look at the lead up to bedtime. Work out a routine that suits you, preferably including a warm bath or shower (to relax and also for a more comfortable sleep), a hot, soothing drink, and some quiet and calming activities. I like to spend a few minutes reflecting on what went right during my day, what I need to do less of, and what I need to do tomorrow. Generally, I have planned the following day well before my bedtime ritual, however, as I don't want to be stressing out on a screen, messaging people and so on, last thing before bed.

4. Try lying with your legs up against a wall for a few minutes. This is a very relaxing pose that is known to aid sleep.

5. If you need some extra help, consider natural sleep aids like valerian, chamomile, magnesium, or melatonin. Putting on some relaxing MHZ sounds on Youtube, and setting my phone to turn off after about an hour is one of my favorite ways to unwind. Sound therapy is a proven way to reduce negativity, relax, and heal. It is very easy to fall asleep to.

6. Avoid big meals right before bed. Rather, stick to healthy, light snacks if you really need something to eat before bed.

7. If you do tend to wake up in the middle of the night use a system to reset sleep, such as any of the tips below.

   1. Whatever you do, do not touch your cellphone or turn on the TV or computer.

   2. Get up out of bed and sit somewhere quietly. Reading, journaling, making lists, or meditation are all good options if you have to do something with this time. Keep the lights dim, but not so dim you will strain your eyes if reading.

   3. When you feel tired again, go back to bed.

If all else fails check in to a sleep clinic and let the experts see if they can identify the issue. Sometimes sleep apnea, pain, or some other health issue can get in the way of good sleep, and may be fairly easy to sort out once the root problem is known.

PRACTICAL EXERCISE: BASICS TRACKING

The best place to start is to simply observe yourself for a week or two. Sometimes what we 'think' we are doing is not quite the same as what is actually happening.

You can put these factors into a table or checklist and keep it on the fridge or by your bed, or track yourself in a notebook, or even on your phone if you prefer. These are the things you need to be making a note of:

1. Time asleep & sleep quality.
2. What you ate.
3. What you drank.
4. Outdoor time or exposure to natural light.
5. Movement/exercise level (1-3). What did you do?
6. Bowel movement/s?
7. Pain/discomfort – where, how much (1-3)?
8. Average stress level (1-3).
9. Average energy level (1-3).
10. Main emotional state for the day.
11. Other – ie: medications taken, menstrual cycle or illness.

Using a standard scale of 1-3 helps you rate each category for consistency's sake: 1 being not at all, 2 being somewhat/average, and 3 being high/a lot.

Once you have the data, decide which area of your life you want to target first. Don't try to change everything at once, though. Pick one priority at a time and work at that until it becomes more habitual.

SETTING HEALTHY HABITS

As mentioned it is best to only attempt setting one habit at a time. If you, like many others, battle with changing habits or creating new ones, use the following tips to help you.

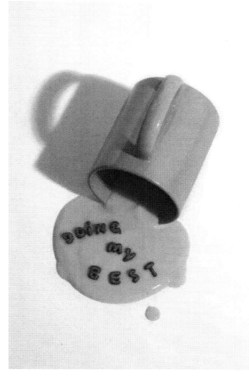

1. If you want to stop a bad habit, you need to have something else to replace it with.

2. Habits are best started in the morning, when you have more energy and less decision fatigue.

3. Start small, pick the smallest, least objectionable level of the new thing. For example, if five minutes of walking around raises no inner resistance, start with that. You want to get the basic action set first, and then you can add extra time and complexity.

4. Consider triggers and rewards. What comes right before the action that signals your brain that it is time to do the thing, and what is (or will) reward it. Rewards are more powerful if they are immediate and sensory-based. Keep your triggers and rewards as consistent as possible (that is, they must be the same thing every time).

5. You can bundle habits together if you wish. If you already have a habit you wish to keep, say it is taking a shower as soon as you wake up, you can bundle hydration with it by drinking a glass of water before you step into the shower. Look at those things you already do daily and consistently, and consider what can be bundled together. This basically means you ride the new habit off an existing one, which makes it easier and faster to habituate.

6. If you skip a day don't think it is all over. Just keep beginning again if you have to. One miss does not mean a failure at all; we are going for an average over time. Of course, the more consistent you can be, the quicker the habit will set.

There is no specific time frame for setting new habits. It depends on consistency, complexity, and the strength of the reward, mostly. You will know the new habit is set when you go to do it automatically, without too much effort, mental resistance, or even that much thought. At that time you can choose the next healthy habit to start on.

PRACTICAL EXERCISE: PRIORITIZING CHANGES

Looking at your daily choices, and now knowing how habits work, what needs to be habituated? What can be easily changed now, and what can be further down the list?

Health/Lifestyle Goals (be specific)	Priority #	Is this a one-off action or a habit I need?	Resources Needed	How else can I support this shift?

Get all the quick and easy stuff done as soon as possible. For example, setting up your room for better sleep is a one-off thing to do. Start on your list. You will find as each new healthy habit strengthens, it has a positive, knock-on effect on all other parts of your life. As you get slowly stronger, overall, this whole process gets easier.

QUICK FIXES FOR ANXIETY

There is quite a bit of research now into how to circumvent the brain entirely and use the body-brain link to directly access and manage our mental state and mood, without having to engage too much with our thoughts.

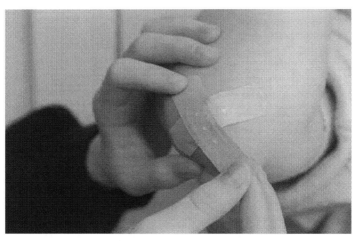

Quick fixes to try when you feel anxious include:

1. Fifteen minutes of brisk activity of any sort.

2. Purposeful body shaking. Shake your arms, hands, legs, and feet. Jiggle your torso. Do this for around five minutes.

3. Dance, whirl or twirl.

4. Move your eyes from side to side for twenty moves, and then look back and up, as if trying to look into the back of your own skull.

5. Use acupressure points by firmly (but gently) pushing the back of a pencil or blunt object, or your finger, into any of the following points for a few minutes each. You can also rub each area in a circular massage motion:

    1. The spot in between your eyebrows.

    2. The top hollow of your ear where it curls in slightly as it nears your head.

    3. In between your thumb and forefinger, on the webbing there.

    4. Your inner arm, about three fingers in from the wrist.

Ayurveda, acupuncture and many other modalities support similar body-brain bypasses. It may be best to use these in moments of high anxiety and to also do the cognitive work required to process complicated or unhelpful thoughts and feelings over time.

WHAT TO DO IF YOU HAVE A PANIC ATTACK

Unmanaged anxiety can ultimately lead to burn out and possibly even full-blown panic attacks. Once you have had one of these extremely unpleasant experiences, you then often find yourself getting anxious that another one might be on its way.

Leading up to a panic attack your body will start giving signs such as numbness, pins and needles, dizziness, shakiness, sweating, pounding heart and pulse, a choking feeling as if you can't breathe, a need to pee, or pain in your stomach. Once having experienced a panic attack, any similar sensations could prime you to panic again. Even if you weren't headed for an attack, you think and scare yourself into one.

In the middle of a panic attack you may feel:

1. Helpless
2. Like the feelings are bigger and more powerful than you.
3. Embarrassed and out of control or as though you are being judged by onlookers.
4. Scared;you don't know what will happen next and it is very frightening.
5. As if time stops. The attack seems to last forever, when in fact most attacks are no longer than around 20 minutes or so.
6. When you are in it, it might feel like you are in danger of a heart attack, suffocation, or death.

If you have never experienced a panic attack, it is so important to try to have empathy for those who have. Nobody chooses to have full-blown anxiety or panic attacks. If you have experienced this, you will know how utterly awful it feels. People suffering from anxiety are not playacting or seeking attention. They do desperately need attention though, and the right kind, to help them start healing and learning how to self calm.

If you start displaying signs of a panic attack there are several things you can do straightaway to help:

1. Stay in place. Do not try to run or move too quickly as that combined with your breathing rate could cause you to faint. If you are driving, pull over. If you are at work or out in public, find a bench or chair, or sit on the floor if you must. If you can, tell someone what is happening or ask for help. You could even get a medic alert bracelet to alert anyone trying to help you what it is that is happening. A panic attack can be frightening for others too, as they don't know what is going on. But really, your focus in the moment needs to be on yourself and your needs. You can always explain later, if you have to. There is a greater awareness around this, and people can be surprisingly supportive if they know what is going on.
2. If you are able, and don't feel dizzy or faint, do a brisk form of activity in place. If you need to walk it off, take a support buddy with you. This helps get the stress chemicals out of your body faster.

3. Remember that this feels very bad right now, but the worst of it does not last more than around 20 to 30 minutes. If you can sit it out, it will soon be over.

4. Slow your breathing as much as you can. Do 'square' breathing: Picture a square, now breathe up the one side for five seconds, hold along the next side for five, breathe out down the next side for five, and hold again for five seconds on the last stretch.

5. Use your personal mantra. We help you with creating this a bi later in the book.

6. Distract your mind. There is the colors and shapes game, where you think about a red square, a pink circle, a green triangle and so on. You simply pick a color and shape and think about it, seeing it in your mind's eye. Or you can focus on an object in front of you and notice its shape, color, smell, texture and so on.

Panic attacks can be beaten. As you work your way through these exercises you will find that all the techniques add up, like building blocks. Each exercise, each tool, contributes to many small shifts that add up into a greater shift towards calm, inner peace and healing.

HOLISTIC ANXIETY FIXES

There is no arguing with the fact that the following methods have been proven time and again to be of great help with managing moods. Increasingly, therapists and counselors are turning to these modalities, and they are becoming more recognized and part of mainstream treatments for people suffering from a variety of problems, including anxiety and panic attacks.

ACUPUNCTURE AND ACUPRESSURE

Acupuncture and acupressure have been used quite successfully for many hundreds, if not thousands, of years. In the ancient Far East, energy lines running throughout the body were used to clear a whole variety of mental, physical and emotional problems.

Scientists can see how these ancient meridians do in fact align with what we now know about our nervous system. There are many points on the body where you can apply your own simple acupressure (firm pressure on a specific spot) if needed. Acupuncture, which uses very fine needles and truly doesn't hurt a bit, is best left to a trained professional to do. Both practices can go a long way to calming an overactive, hypervigilant system, and healing any physical imbalances that may be contributing to anxiety levels as well.

YOGA

Gentle stretching is one of my favorite ways to wind down right before bed. Yoga is therapeutic for the body and the mind. It helps you learn how to control your breath, and also encourages a quieter mind. focusing on each yoga position is enough to keep a usually active brain quiet for a period of time, too.

PSYCHEDELIC THERAPY

The anti-drug movement has calmed down a little, and therapists and the science community are beginning to recognize and use various psychedelics as a way to heal people with depression, anxiety, addictions, and PTSD, amongst other ailments. When used in a clinical context, and with verifiably clean, pure substances, the risk is seen to be quite low (Robertson, 2021). This type of therapy can fast-track the healing process if done correctly. There needs to be a therapeutic lead-up, and debrief, and a trained professional needs to be present at all times to ensure that things go smoothly.

Patients have reported achieving results equal to many years of therapy in one psychedelic session. It is believed that the various psychedelic substances used help the brain to reset itself in many instances, fast-tracking neural healing, neurogenesis, and correcting neural pathways.

CALM, SAFE SPACES

If possible, have a place where you can be quiet and where you feel safe. For children I create a calm corner at home, where there are soft, squishy beanbags, books, cool colors like blues and greens, and soft music they can play if they wish. When someone is in the calm space, no one is allowed to interrupt them.

Having your own calm space might sound like a dream, especially if you have a large, busy family, pets and so on, but give it a try! Encourage everyone else in your household to also do the same, and teach and encourage self-managed time outs.

We all need a few moments where no one is asking us to do something, or where we can limit sensory input for a bit; a space that triggers our parasympathetic nervous system, that triggers happy, good feelings.

MEDITATION

Research on the benefits of meditation and how it works to calm an anxious brain has been slowly gathering impetus for years. Using fMRI and EEG we can see differences in the brain activity of frequent meditators versus those who don't practice any form of meditation. Meditation increases grey matter (neurons, connections between them, and neural regenesis). It also helps us master our moods and put our focus where we want it to be, rather than allowing our minds to be the masters of us.

A Yale University study showed that meditation calms what is known as the 'monkey mind', reducing activity in those parts of the brain that are responsible for 'mind-wandering'. This random type of thought is associated with worrying, stress, overthinking and so on, so the more control we have over it, and the quicker we can snap out of this mode, the better for our anxiety levels (Walton, 2015).

Meditation helps train your brain and strengthen your ability to manage your focus, thoughts and moods.

PRACTICAL EXERCISE: SIMPLE MEDITATION FOR BEGINNERS

You don't need to be the Dalai Lama to enjoy the benefits of meditation. The following are some basic tips for how to get started:

1. Get comfortable. Make sure your clothes aren't restrictive and sit or lie however you wish that feels good for you.
2. Set your cellphone on a timer for the lowest amount of time that you feel okay with. If that's only two or three minutes at first that is fine. You just don't want to worry about what the time is during your meditation.
3. With your eyes open (if possible), focus your vision on something in front of you that is not that exciting to look at and is not moving about. This is just a focal point, really. I suggest practicing with eyes open as in real-life you will find it easier to slip into a highly calm, focused state no matter what you are doing. You can't always close your eyes in traffic or

that boardroom meeting, but you do want to be able to access the calm state as needed.

4. Now, just breathe slowly, and for each breath count. Counting is reflexive and you shouldn't need to think about it that much, so it is a good way to keep your mind busy with very little conscious effort.

5. If thoughts creep in, which they will with our delightful monkey minds, gently push them to one side, and start counting from one again. If you really can't push them aside, write them down on a piece of paper, and then continue meditating.

6. Reward yourself at the end with tea and a biscuit or something physically rewarding for you. Ultimately, meditation is its own reward and becomes self-reinforcing once you start feeling the benefits of the amazing calmness it brings. If you fall asleep now and then, that's okay too. Don't be too critical of what happens, especially in the beginning.

It's as simple as that. After a few days of even a couple of minutes' meditation per day, you will start noticing a difference in your levels of stress and also in your ability to focus on things. Keep going. Meditation should be like brushing your teeth: It is an important part of your mental hygiene.

As you become more habituated, you can add extra minutes to your regular meditations. You can also vary your practice with walking meditation, guided meditations, or by using different focal points like a lit candle or inspirational visual.

MINDFUL LIVING

Training your mind to focus on what is in front of it right now, in this moment, is a great way to lessen anxiety. Mindfulness is learned by repeated practice. We live in an age where we tend to practice distraction and worry more than anything. We easily slip into regrets or guilt over the past, or worry about the future, or let our minds wander all over the place distracted by any number of things around us. It's not the things themselves that are the problem, it is how we are allowing ourselves to behave in relation to the world.

Bearing in mind that we have probably been practicing distraction and worry for a large part of our lives, we now need to start putting some real energy into the opposite: mindfulness!

PRACTICAL EXERCISE: MINDFULNESS

Take a few minutes every day to start training yourself into a more mindful way of being, with the following tips as your guide:

1. Focus on your senses: What can you see, taste, touch, hear, feel, or smell? Really drop into the moment and gently push any other thoughts to one side. Dinnertime is a good time to try this as you can focus on each bite, each movement, each taste and sensation.
2. Find something you love doing, whether that is trail running, painting, or anything in between. When you are able to lose yourself in a hobby or activity, time seems to stand still or become meaningless as your focus sharpens onto only that which matters in the moment.
3. Put a reminder on your phone or a printout on your wall; something that will prompt you to focus on this moment and to observe what state of mind you are in regularly.

With time, this mindfulness muscle will strengthen.

There are many other ways to help train your mind to calm and focus itself, like yoga, sporting activities, art and creative pursuits and so on. Find your thing and practice it often.

CHAPTER 3:
THE MIND AS A TOOL

· · · · · · · · · · · · · · ·

Unless we take a moment to think about it fully, we often confuse how we are feeling with who we are and with what is happening. Our feelings can feel bigger than us, like a life sentence, and can become completely overwhelming if we let them. If we more clearly understand what our feelings are, we are less easily led down this path. By learning about, and engaging with, our feelings, we can master them rather than us being mastered and controlled by them.

A well-known guru, Sadhguru, explains how our minds are like tools. If we are simply handed a tool, like a knife for example, we might not have any idea how to use it safely. We may hurt ourselves by holding it the wrong way. And so many of us do; we end up frustrated, stressed, anxious, and depressed.

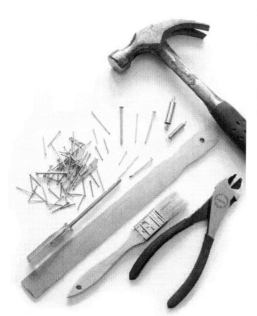

So how do we learn how to use this tool safely?

WHAT ARE FEELINGS?

Where do feelings come from? What are they? Well, feelings on a basic, scientific level are caused by chemicals released by our brains and bodies. These chemicals, like adrenaline, can make our heartbeats race, or, like oxytocin, can make us bond with others and feel calm.

But what causes these chemicals to be released in the first place?

Generally, this release is either based on a physical issue, an illness or imbalance. For example, too much sugar can inflame the brain, too much caffeine can overstimulate it, or a hormonal imbalance can release a whole chemical storm within us. This can be misinterpreted as a feeling that is based on what is happening to us environmentally, rather than what is happening inside of us physically. So a woman with bad PMS (and the resulting chemical fluctuations) may feel irritable and interpret this as her life externally being a problem, rather than the internal mechanism it really is.

The other reason we may be feeling a certain way is that we have thought our way into specific feelings. Something happens in our lives, we have certain thoughts about the situation, and these thoughts are what trigger our brains to release the chemicals that create the feeling.

This is perhaps a simplistic way to explain it, but it is basically what you need to know to understand that feelings themselves are not an end result or necessarily true; they are merely indicators, or messengers, that either something physical needs attention (those basics we spoke about earlier), or we need to look at the quality of our thoughts and what part of our environment may need adjusting.

When we are feeling bad, there are three questions we need to ask ourselves:

1. Am I tired, hungry, ill, or might there be some other simply remedied physical reason I am feeling off?
2. What am I feeling? What thoughts was I thinking right before I felt sad, bad, angry, anxious, etc.?
3. What is happening when I think these thoughts? Is there something in my life situation that could be adjusted?

We have already dealt fairly thoroughly with point one. So let's take a look at properly identifying our feelings next.

SELF AWARENESS

Some of us battle to name our feelings. It's not that we couldn't if we knew how, it is just that often we aren't encouraged to engage with our feelings that much. There has been a toxic social norm historically that discourages us from engaging with our feelings as showing them is seen as weak, overly emotional, and negative. Unfortunately, this avoidance means that we don't learn to identify and use feelings as the tools they truly are. We are thus unable to see ourselves clearly. This ultimately disconnects us from ourselves, from others, and also from our healing and growth.

Self awareness starts with being aware of our thoughts and feelings, and how these influence our choices and actions. It leads to greater self-confidence, empathy, better social interactions and relationships, emotional maturity, and increased self-control and self-management on all levels.

If feelings could talk, what might they be saying?

1. Anger might be telling you that:
2. you are scared.
3. you are ashamed.
4. you feel threatened.
5. there is something you want that you are not getting.
6. your sense of fairness/rightness/justice is being challenged.
7. your boundaries are being pushed.
8. Depression might be telling you that you need a break (deep rest), or that there is something wrong that you are not facing or expressing to yourself or others.
9. Loneliness might be telling you to create more meaningful connections, either with yourself, others, a higher power, nature, or even a pet.
10. Resentment might be letting you know that you need to forgive.
11. Emptiness or lack of motivation and interest in life may mean you need to do something creative or purposeful/meaningful to you.
12. Anxiety and stress may be asking you to simplify your life.
13. Worry may be indicating to you that you are living in an unknown future and must work to make it as known as you can. Analyse the facts and risks and make some plans.
14. Shame may mean you need more self-compassion. If you did wrong, take the lesson, make what amends you can, and start the healing.
15. Regret may mean you are living in the past. Unless you have a time machine, you cannot change it, so take the lesson and move on.
16. Sadness may mean you need to allow your grief in, and express it.

PRACTICAL EXERCISE: WHAT AM I FEELING?

Every day at around the same time, take mental stock by asking yourself the following:

1. What has been my primary emotion in the last 24 hours?
2. How do I feel right now?
3. Where do I feel this emotion in my body?
4. What need might this feeling be linked to and what do I need to do right now?

If you are unsure of any of the answers, there are some great infographics showing facial expressions linked to feelings (emojis), to help you get more specific.

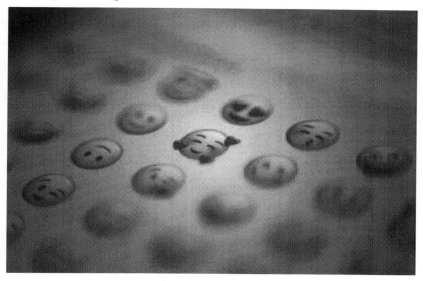

Make a habit of checking in with yourself, and, if you wish, start linking the emotion to the underlying message it is trying to share with you.

If you want you could visualize emotions like large, friendly dogs with a mission. Is little Jimmy down the well? Is there a ball that needs throwing or catching? Does someone need a tummy rub or dinner? Engage with them as helpful messengers and see the difference this makes in how you work with them and yourself.

Of course, sometimes the messenger dog is Winston Churchill's black dog of gloom, or a terrifying rottweiler, but you can still learn how to read the message and perhaps even train them to heel on command.

OBSERVING OUR THOUGHTS

We, the totality of who we are, is made up of all the things we have learned, experienced, been taught and told, since birth. These create our core beliefs about the world and what it is all about.

If you realize that each person has their own unique set of experiences and learnings, then you understand that there is a vast variety of ways we each engage with and think about life. Sometimes these are useful, helpful and constructive, but sometimes we may have picked up less useful core beliefs and habits of thinking.

You will only know which category your core beliefs fall into if you take some time to examine the quality of your thoughts.

PRACTICAL EXERCISE: WATCH YOUR THOUGHTS

Over time, if you pay attention, you can pick up patterns of thought and then examine them more easily once you have clearly established what they are.

1. Carry a pencil and notebook around with you.

2. When anything goes wrong, or you feel bad, take a quick moment to note what you are thinking and what happened.

3. After a week or so of this, take a look at your notes. Do you see any pattern of events and thoughts?

4. Sometimes it is obvious that events are not ideal. Perhaps you have a toxic family member or work colleague, or perhaps a recurring situation is triggering or difficult to handle? This is where you decide what needs changing.

    1. Can you see what is not working or what you need to do more or less of?

2. Can you avoid the problem or get help to better understand and change it?

5. Even when the events or outside circumstances aren't great (and often we cannot do much about how other people behave), there is a lot we can do about how we think about and react to them. If you notice that your thoughts are regularly fairly negative, how can you reframe them so that they don't result in such bad feelings?

Here are a few examples of ways to do so:

My usual negative thought is...	I can reframe it this way...
I can't get anything right.	Sometimes I make mistakes, but I am learning every day.
Why is this happening to me?/ Bad things always happen to me.	This is happening. What can I do about it?
What is wrong with me?	I am working on myself. How can I do better?
I am such a loser.	Sometimes bad things happen, and I can learn from them and keep getting stronger.
I can't do this.	I notice I feel overwhelmed. I have managed to get through 100% of everything before; I can also get through this.

Simply turning a negative thought into its opposite is not enough. It is unlikely that your subconscious will accept that, as it does not make sense to you and what you have been thinking up until now. So a better way to reframe negative thoughts is to shift the thought into a more constructive one that you can accept.

Now, for your next trick, you need to keep watching your thoughts and when you catch a negative inner voice breaking you down, consistently reframe it. These negative inner tapes are often untrue and definitely unhelpful. The more often we catch and challenge them, the less often they will occur. Over time they will grow weaker and less able to influence us. As the quality of our thoughts improves, we will find ourselves feeling stronger and less anxious.

FAULTY THINKING

We all want to believe that we are using a fair amount of logic and rational thought, but sometimes we cannot see ourselves as clearly as we may like. There are some common cognitive distortions we are all fairly subject to. Many of them are due to the fact that our brains do some strange things in their efforts to make sense of the world.

Unless we are aware of these cognitive distortions, we cannot guard against them. Take a look at the following and consider where you may be falling into these misleading thought traps.

1. Confirmation Bias is when we pay more attention to any new information that confirms what we think we already know, and filter out anything that contradicts it. It stops us from truly hearing and engaging with any opposing views or considering them objectively.
2. Hindsight Bias is when we look back on situations and believe "we knew it all along", when in fact we actually weren't sure until it happened. This tends to push us to look for similar patterns and then predict outcomes based on past hindsights we have had.
3. Anchoring Bias is when we hear one fact and then anchor all our further thoughts and decisions on that, rather than giving all new facts equal consideration. A good example is when we are influenced by the first impression we have of others.
4. False Consensus is our tendency to believe that others think and feel the same way we do. We expect them to agree, and when they don't, we view this as intentionally being foolish, wrong, bad, etc. In fact, we are all just different, and if we can be more open to these differences it might create space for deeper mutual understanding.

5. Self-serving, or Victim Mentality, is when we take credit for our successes, but blame failures on others or outside events. Locus of Control is another term therapists like to use. This is when we feel we have control over our lives, which is an Inner Locus of Control. An External Locus of Control means that we feel powerless and that life happens to us. Others are then always to blame and never ourselves. The problem is that, with this logic, we can never own our problems, and then we can't take the steps we need to grow, learn or improve.

There are many other ways our minds can trick us, and so it pays to get as many facts as we can, and question our core beliefs and thoughts frequently. When it comes to anxiety, we may find that once we unpack unhelpful core beliefs and faulty thinking, we strengthen ourselves and become less susceptible to irrational fears and triggers.

PRACTICAL EXERCISE: IDENTIFYING FAULTY THINKING

Consider times in your life when any of the above thought patterns have misled you. Reflect on what happened, what your thoughts and choices were and what you could have done differently.

1. Is there an area of your life where you consistently hit a brick wall?

    1. Do you have all the facts? Where else might you find more information? Make a pros and cons list, or simply list all the facts that you have, and then make a good attempt to add to them with some solid research on all sides of the situation.

    2. Is there a mentor or person you trust, who has no investment or agenda in the issue, that you can discuss the situation with?

    3. Is there something you can do more of, or less of, or avoid, that might change things for the better?

WATCH YOUR FOCUS

Controlling your mind is not about forcing it. That simply does not work. Think about your mind as a vast map of places: You have a place for thoughts about family, work, home, chores, hobbies, health, all kinds of things really. Now your focus is where you choose to shine the light of your attention. If you are continually shining your attention onto sad, upsetting, dark places in your mind, that is what you will mostly be seeing, thinking about, and thus, feeling.

This does not mean we do not engage with stuff in our life that needs attention. There is no doubt we need to look at issues, allow our feelings, use them to point us towards what parts of our lives need attention and make whatever plans we need to, to shift things into a better state. But once we have done all of those things, we need to then learn how to put our focus elsewhere.

Continuously focusing on negative thoughts means that our energy and attention is trained there. The thoughts then grow in strength and power in our minds, and will obviously make us feel bad.

Practicing meditation and the other focus-strengthening exercises that we've already mentioned,is one way to improve our focusing skills. Another way is just to stay mindful of where we are allowing our focus to go, and to actively shift it off the stuff we don't want and onto more uplifting, motivating, and useful areas of our lives.

This is not as simple as to just think positively. That does not typically work, if we haven't fully dealt with the issue our focus keeps shifting back to, or are in the habit of mentally going there ourselves. It's more about purposely distracting ourselves as best we can. Think about it like watching a movie. When you watch an action, comedy or horror movie, the director skillfully directs your attention onto what they want, and in the process you feel sad, happy, excited, scared and so forth. This, by the way, is a normal function of the subconscious, that does not distinguish between real and unreal, and simply records and is influenced by what is visually placed before it.

It's just the same with where you focus your mind in terms of memories, core beliefs and so on. Be the director of your own movie and your own life and mind. Choose where you put your focus, and, as a consequence, you choose the feelings that are the result.

CHAPTER 4:
REPROGRAMMING THE SYSTEM

I f you have been in the habit of feeling anxious for quite some time, you are going to need to be gentle and patient with yourself. Feeling calmer, happier, and more at ease is possible, and if you have already been engaging with the exercises in this workbook, they should be having some positive effect.

But of course, we will not leave it there when there is so much more you can do to have the quality of life you want.

Let's learn and apply a few extra skills to help you level up even more.

CORE BELIEFS

These are things we have decided are true in our lives. Again, we all have a variety of them, different from other people's core beliefs. Some of us may have a set of core beliefs that are less useful, and we will only know this if we can unpack what they are.

PRACTICAL EXERCISE: WHAT AM I THINKING?

In any given situation, you will have core beliefs that influence your thoughts, feelings and thus your actions. If you know what underlies it all, you can start reframing or shifting them, particularly if they aren't that helpful for you.

When you find yourself having a thought, usually about yourself, other people, or a situation, ask yourself a series of 'whys'. Put it in this format:

I think....

Why?

For each answer, ask why again until you feel like you have got to the root of the issue. Then challenge that thought, question it, and look for other information that might give you more or different insight into what you originally thought.

REWRITING YOUR STORY

The narrative of your life and all the things that have happened to you, especially the bad stuff, can be told in many ways without changing any of the base facts or reality.

Rewriting your story does not mean you need to twist the truth or deceive yourself. In reality, cognitive studies show that we do, in any case, always apply our own filters and interpretations onto everything we see, hear and experience. That is why one car crash viewed by 20 different people will generally elicit 20 different stories. Each person has their own cognitive bias.

Research shows that how we interpret things can also be nudged, tweaked and changed by the person interviewing us. This has been taken as far as inserting false memories into people's minds through suggestion, leading questions, and various other cognitive methods (Loftus, 2019).

The brain is not a recording device, it is a survival machine. Left to its own devices, it will put whatever interpretation on the facts that it needs to, to make the narrative easier for the person to deal with. While the subconscious does record whatever it 'sees', it also records everything you, as the thinker, repeatedly feeding it.

This is why negative self-talk can be so destructive. It is a continual loop of harsh self-doubt and criticism that programs us for failure. And the irony is that these negative inner tapes are often things others have said to us, or faulty cognitive conclusions we have drawn that aren't even true. We have already dealt with that to a large degree earlier in this workbook.

Similarly to negative self-talk, the stories we tell ourselves over and over about our lives can be very harmful and self-destructive too. If we can identify what these stories are, and reframe them to be more constructive and supportive of ourselves, we have a better chance of feeling better overall.

PRACTICAL EXERCISE: REFRAME THE NARRATIVE

If you can, do this exercise as a handwritten process. This engages a more analytical part of the brain and also helps you reflect on what you are thinking and see it in black-and-white.

1. Think back to as many major events or memories as you can. Perhaps even put them in a timeline and, using keywords, summarize what happened, what you thought and what you felt. Also add what you feel about that memory now.

2. Choose one of the events, and break it down.

   1. Who was involved?

   2. What happened?

   3. What were your thoughts and feelings at the time?

   4. How old were you?

   5. How has that memory affected you now, in your current life choices?

3. Looking at this memory through adult, or current, eyes, is there any way to interpret what happened differently?

4. What would an unrelated observer have seen, do you think?

5. Now look at how you are telling the story. Is there another way to phrase it that is less upsetting, and more empowering for you?

Example #1:

Original Narrative

When I was five, my mom smacked me hard on the hand and told me I was uncontrollable. I still feel anger and resentment when I think about it.

Reframed

When I was five I grabbed a power cord and nearly hurt myself. My mom and I both reacted with fear and anger. She could have handled that better, but she was trying to keep me safe. I don't have to like her methods, but I can understand her intention.

Example #2:

Original Narrative

I was kept back a grade when I was 11. I felt stupid, and all the other kids teased me.

Reframed

I may have been struggling with the emotional and mental demands of the grade. I did start school quite early. Staying back a grade gave me a chance to consolidate my learning, and today I am doing well in life anyway.

Can you see how one story can make you feel pretty bad, but reframed and without changing any facts, you can remember it a bit more constructively, and without having to repeat the original bad feelings over and over again?

For more traumatic memories, it may be advisable to get external assistance from a professional counsellor who can provide you with support and help you process the feelings and reframe the story. Sometimes these memories and feelings can be too big for us to handle on our own.

DEALING WITH FEAR AND WORRY

A large part of anxiety can be based on worry about an unknown future, about what might happen, and whether we will be able to handle it or not.

Making the unknown known is a really good way to help calm these fears. Once you have more clarity, you can then put contingency plans in place. Having that thought out in advance gives you a sense of control and preparedness. It helps lessen your worries immensely.

PRACTICAL EXERCISE: DEFINING YOUR WORRIES

Again, do this as a written exercise. This is really just a basic risk analysis, but it works well in helping us name our fears.

1. Draw a large square and separate it into four quadrants.
2. On the bottom left write 'unlikely to happen' and on the top left write 'highly likely'.
3. On the bottom right write 'low impact' and on the far right write 'high impact'.
4. Now brainstorm all the things that can possibly go wrong in your life. Don't judge these thoughts, just write them down. Nobody is going to see this except you.
5. Each worry will have a place to go in one of the quadrants: Either it will be unlikely, and if it happens it won't really have a big impact; it will be likely but still not have a big impact on your life; it will be unlikely but could have a big impact on you; and lastly, it is quite likely to happen and if it does it will be a serious problem for you.
6. The worries you put in the last quadrant are the ones you need to deal with first.

Problem/ Worry	What can I do to head this off?	What can I do if it happens?	What resources might I need, or who could assist me?

Taking the unknown and making it known, and thus practically more easy to plan for as needed, helps you relax a little.

While using mindfulness, meditation, and techniques to focus your attention on the present moment is key to reducing anxiety, you still need to deal with the practicalities of possible future needs, as well as processing and releasing guilt or concerns about the past. Eckhardt Tolle speaks at length about this in his book *The Power of Now*, and succinctly explains how when we allow our minds to remain pointlessly in some unknown, uncertain future, we create anxiety based on an illusion. The illusion is one of both imagination and time. By allowing our minds to wander into an unknown future, we create all kinds of imagined problems. Often these imaginations are about situations that never happen. But we cause ourselves as much anxiety and worry as if they were happening right now.

So, once you have analyzed all realistic future risks and made whatever plans or taken whatever steps are necessary to head off the likely problems, it is best to let these thoughts go. There is nothing further you can practically do about a possible-yet-not-definite future event except cause yourself unnecessary pain.

If, after all of these exercises, you still find yourself battling to move your focus back into the present moment, a good question that will also help you gain some perspective and reduce anxiety is:

"Is there a problem I need to deal with at this moment?"

If your answer is no, focus your attention on what there is to enjoy and be grateful for right now. Keep your focus there, and your worries will become less significant, especially if you have done what you can about them in preparation. There is then nothing more to do than to experience and enjoy this moment. After all, the past has happened; you can't go back and change it. The future is not definite; you can prepare for some of it but not all. Only this moment is what you have direct knowledge of, and maybe some control over. Your life is made up of each moment, second by second, and if you spend it with your mind wandering around in time and never fully present, you will miss it.

Bringing your awareness into what is in front of you, or merely being aware that you have not been aware, helps you practice the skill of present consciousness. The more you do this, the more you find inner peace as the gaps between conscious presence and unconscious mental ramblings grow more, and you stay more easily in the moment.

If there is a problem in this moment, then it is easy to make decisions and take action, and that very situation helps take your focus off the worry and onto a more empowered feeling of self-determination.

If you find yourself going into fight-flight-freeze mode, especially feeling frozen, stuck or overwhelmed, a great mantra to try is:

"Although this is not ideal, I will be okay."

Most day-to-day problems are not life threatening, and the reminder that you have survived and managed 100% of all previous problems (otherwise you would not be here now, still alive and surviving) is a great reminder that you can do so again, no matter what the challenge.

DEALING WITH CHALLENGES

Sometimes life throws you a curveball. Whatever it is, we could slip into unhelpful patterns of thought, and react emotionally in ways that are perhaps unhelpful or destructive. A better option is to apply the three Ws:

1. Wait. Even if it is just for half an hour, if you can delay your response it is always best. Why? Because you need to give your body and brain the chance to process the fight-flight-freeze chemicals and to allow your higher thinking to kick back in. Even if you think you are fine, in most cases your root, animal

brain and stress chemicals like adrenaline will be having an effect. And that means no matter how logical you think you are being at the moment, chances are that you are not.

If there is any way to remove yourself, delay, or defer your next move, take it. Use some brisk activity to process the stress chemicals out of your system faster.

Of course, if the issue is a real physical threat, like snatching your child out of oncoming traffic, or dodging a brick someone just threw at you, then the quick actions your adrenaline and other fight-flight chemicals support are perfect to use in the moment. The very actions you need to take to save yourself or those around you will use up the chemicals, and afterwards you will be able to calm yourself faster anyway in order to take next steps.

2. What. What actions do you need to take to solve the immediate problem? Do you need to ask for help, talk things through, make a plan or new goal for yourself? Getting into constructive action is far better than sitting frozen, disempowered and helpless.

3. Welcome change. Gather as many facts as you can about what happened, and consider what needs to change. No matter what has happened, there is generally a lesson you can take from it. What could you have done differently? What can you do more or less to avoid a repeat of the problem? By being open to change you become more flexible and adaptable. Those who refuse to adapt eventually don't make it. We see that in nature and evolution. If you stay stuck in a comfort zone, it grows increasingly uncomfortable as life shifts around you until eventually there is some sort of breakdown of you (or the system), and then hopefully a breakthrough that leads to positive change. To avoid big breakdowns, being open to continual small shifts and changes helps keep life fresh, interesting, adaptive, and mostly stress-free.

The definition of failure is not never trying at all, or trying and then giving up. If you can keep going and get up each time life knocks you down, you strengthen your resilience and all the skills that go with that.

This does not mean to keep doing something that is clearly not working; it instead means to keep asking the questions, adapting, and putting energy into your next best step.

"Success consists of getting up just one more time than you fall." – Oliver Goldsmith

PRACTICAL EXERCISE: FACING CHALLENGES

1. Accept that there will be challenges. Getting stuck in resistance to what is happening does not help you effectively deal with the situation at hand. When you feel frustrated, angry or defensive, ask yourself if you are simply resisting what is?
2. Are you able to drop that feeling of resistance and replace it with a feeling of curiosity? Asking questions like why, what, when, how, with what, by when, and who, can all give you clarity around the issue. A simple 5-why problem-solving process is also useful. All you do is keep asking 'why' until you feel you have arrived at the root cause of the problem. Then it becomes easier to decide what to do next.
3. Try mindmapping the problem. Write it in the centre of a page and circle it. Then draw lines off of it to any related ideas, resources, contributing factors, and circle each of those. Keep going, unpacking your thoughts on paper to help you get clarity. Sometimes this helps you realize elements that were hidden by the 'noise' before, or creatively unpack possible next steps and needs.

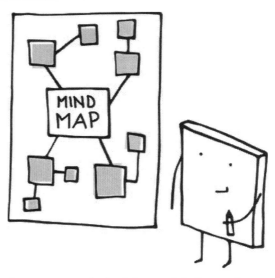

4. Once you have as much insight and information as you can, then decide your action plan. What needs to happen, in what order, by when, with whose help, etc?

5. Lastly, reflect on what you have learned. Write it down or journal it. Discuss it with a mentor. Is there any way you can use this information to leverage future successes or self-growth?

When we are faced with hard times, it does not feel good. But now you know that these feelings are not who you are, they are just messengers that indicate that you need to be paying attention to something or doing something differently. We know that life is made up of good times and bad times. How you manage yourself and your feelings, using all the great CBT tools I have given you, will make all the difference between falling apart inside or building an internal resilience to stand up one more time and say, "It's okay. I can do this!"

COMPLEXITY VS SIMPLICITY

When there is just too much going on, or going wrong, it is easy to feel overwhelmed. Often my clients sit in tears, explaining all the parts of their lives, work, home and relationships that are challenging them in their current life situation. They are so deep in the chaos of it, they can't see the wood for the trees. The very first thing a person in this situation needs to do is to simplify.

What complexity can be cut from your life, right now, that will provide immediate relief? If you don't take the time to declutter, the pressure builds. If you also don't have any way to process and release the emotions that go with that, you are at risk of that pressure resulting in some form of explosion. That can take the form of panic attacks, burn out, breakdowns and so on.

PRACTICAL EXERCISE: DECLUTTERING AND SIMPLIFYING

What is happening in your life right now that is contributing to your anxiety?

Sometimes we can feel tired, overwhelmed, panicked, anxious or depressed because we are dragging around thoughts and emotions that are no longer useful. A strong sign of the need to declutter and 'let go' of unhelpful feelings is lowered levels of tolerance, irritability and unusual mood swings and 'out of character' behaviours. These are also common signs of being stuck in an unhelpful comfort zone.

Letting go of those aspects of our lives that no longer work for us can be extremely freeing and healing, but this process can be hard to start. Use this simple guide to help you with the process:

Inventory Range (what might need to be examined/what might need to go)

1. Material possessions (books, clothes, music, furniture, photographs, 'stuff', etc.)
2. Professional possessions (files, paperwork, clubs and societies, responsibilities, contacts, etc.)
3. Living 'possessions' (plants, animals, people that aren't good for you)
4. Emotional or mental 'possessions' like hurts, wounds, reactions, triggers, memories, resentments, stories, limiting beliefs, expectations, opinions, ideas, world views, etc. Any emotional reaction which lasts longer than a minute is also

generally a sign that a bigger hurt or problem needs examination or assistance.

5.   Behavioural 'possessions' linked to the point above, such as habits, routines, reactions and triggers

Think about your life and what drags you down/makes you feel overwhelmed, tired, irritable or anxious. List them in the left column. Then for each thing you identify, answer the questions in the remaining columns.

These are all ways you can start shifting your life to support more inner calm, and reduce your levels of anxiety. Some of the exercises only need to be done once, or perhaps once a month or year. Others you can keep and go back to time and again, as the need arises.

What is dragging me down? (How does it feel when I think about it? Does it feel good or bad?)	Will I keep this or let it go? (What do I want to do?)	If it is going... Physical Clutter: What can I sell, give away, throw away, rehome?	If it is going... Emotional/Mental Clutter: mentally 'let go', create boundaries, forgive, decide, brainstorm, etc.	Next Steps

CHAPTER 5:
MENTAL AND EMOTIONAL HOUSEKEEPING

● ● ● ● ● ● ● ● ● ● ● ● ●

Once you have some of the building blocks in place, like a supportive lifestyle, self-care, mindfulness and awareness around your thoughts and feelings and what to do with them, your anxiety will start to ease exponentially.

As each pebble blocking your way is removed, the trickle grows until the dam of worry and stress drains away, leaving behind a small stream of the more usual anxieties that are easy to manage. It is unlikely that you will ever have a totally stress-free life. However, you can get pretty close. Even when challenges keep presenting themselves you will have built up the mental and emotional muscle needed to maintain inner ease.

To help you achieve that, and maintain it, there are a few things I like to put down to housekeeping: Regular check-ins and activities, just like sweeping and dusting but on another level, that will help you stay in a good mental and emotional space no matter what life throws at you.

KNOW WHO YOU ARE AND WHAT YOU WANT

Sometimes we can go many years without ever asking ourselves who we are or what we really want for ourselves. As children, we are guided as to what our caregivers want, which may or may not be aligned to our own identities or needs. As we grow, we are guided by our teachers, friends, work colleagues, social or cultural norms, and so on. People will tell us in well-meaning ways what they feel is best for us. Most often this is based on their own learning, preferences and limitations. No one can truly know what is best or possible for you except you, and yet quite often we let others weigh in and make decisions about our lives for us.

Here's the thing though: If we are living a life according to everyone else's agenda but our own, we are not living an authentic life. By 'authentic' I mean true to who you are and what is best for you. Not your mother, father, boss, friends, or anyone else, but you.

How do you know what is yours and what is theirs? How do you know what it is you really want?

It starts with knowing what is important to you. These are your values and what will lie behind most of your decisions. There are no right or wrong answers here. As long as you are not harming yourself, or any others in the process, you get to decide what works for you. This is a powerful journey of self-discovery, and frees you from a lot of stuff that was never meant for you in the first place. Bearing in mind that you have limited time on this planet, you should be able to decide how you spend it, right?

For some people that will be adventure, rock-climbing, or skydiving. For others that will be sitting in their garden with a book, writing, or painting. Some will be family people and love gatherings, Sunday lunches, lots of kids, and family outings. Others will prefer to live alone, in a cabin in the forest, with a pet cat. Some will love boardroom battles and corporate strategizing, and others might prefer to work for themselves or have a defined routine job. There is no limit, or standard definition, of what any of this looks like for you.

PRACTICAL EXERCISE: WHAT'S IMPORTANT?

Look at your current life.

1. What daily habits or choices are you making? How might these relate to what is important to you? These need to be freely made actions, decided by you, that also feel good to do. When we feel frustrated, annoyed and grumpy about having to do something, this is an indication it is not aligned with your values. As does the use of the word 'should' or 'should not';

this tells you it is something someone else wants, but not necessarily your choice.

2. What bigger life choices have you made and how might these relate to what is important to you?

Choice	Possible Value
Going to the gym	Health, socializing
Watching TV	Rest, relaxation
Reading your child a bedtime story every night	Relationships, education

These examples should give you some idea of how to connect up what is happening in your life with what you value.

3. Think about values in general. Look up a list of them online; there are many. Values like trust, integrity, freedom, connection, relationships, family, love, honor, truth, rest, fun, sensory pleasure, financial stability, bravery, health, the list goes one. None are right or wrong. They just are. Which ones resonate with you? Make a list, brainstorm it, or select them from an existing list online.

4. Once you have your list use the following table to evaluate them:

My Values	Where in my life is there a conflict between the situation and my values?	How could I align my life choices more closely with this value?

This is a great step towards figuring out who you are and what works and does not work for you. When you live your life according to other people's agendas you tend to feel out of sorts, often anxious and frustrated.

When in doubt, place your hand on your heart and ask yourself:

"What is it in this moment that I want?"

Ask this question as often as you can and feel in your body the emotional response that will tell you if the choice is good or bad for you. Do it for any choice that you feel unsure about. You will literally feel a clear pull towards the idea, or a general bad or unhappy feeling. Go with it, if you can. If you can't, start looking at ways that you can shift your life more closely in alignment with what you want in the future.

BUILDING SELF-WORTH

If our self-worth is shaky, we will lack confidence in ourselves and our choices. We will doubt our strengths and magnify our weaknesses, until we feel unable to make the right decisions or take actions that are needed for our highest good.

This can come from past abuse, whether emotional or physical, and when our belief in ourself has been consistently shaken, or shaken badly enough by a specific bad experience. It can be as innocuous as a parent always doing everything for us which disempowers us and can make us think we are unable or incompetent on our own.

Whatever the reason, low self-worth can affect almost every area of your life, such as:

1. Increased negative self-talk that breaks you down on every level. This can be you saying bad things about yourself out loud as a 'joke', or in your head.
2. Blaming yourself, even when you are not at fault.
3. Believing you don't deserve happiness, success, or pleasure.
4. Giving up your time, energy and resources to others you think are more deserving.
5. Avoiding challenges for fear of failure.
6. Being extra sensitive to failure or criticism.
7. Thinking compliments are not real, but criticisms are always true.
8. Thinking other people are better than you.

9. Being blind to any successes and strengths you have.
10. Feeling depressed, ashamed, worthless and anxious

Do you see how this can severely impact the quality of your life?

The irony is that a low self-worth is almost never based on fact. It is a fiction that others have put into your head. The good news is that you can build your self-worth up again.

Many of the CBT exercises already given in this workbook will start the healing process, particularly the practices of reframing negative thinking and embracing change and challenges.

PRACTICAL EXERCISE: REBUILDING SELF-WORTH

This is not an overnight process, but it is possible. The following exercises will help a lot in the process of rebuilding your self-worth.

1. Stay mindful of any negative things you say about yourself and to yourself. When you catch yourself, challenge this thinking and reframe it. Be stubborn about this and unrelenting. Eventually it does ease and reduce its noxious impact on your life.

2. Put your focus on your successes and strengths.

My achievements in life/today.	What did I contribute to this success?

3. Keep a success journal. Every evening reflect on what you got right on that day and make a short list. Only list good things and achievements as we want to put your focus firmly on successes. Remember that your focus has been on a lot of negative stuff for probably quite some time, so this is not about balance but about healing and strengthening.

   1. Reflect on what perfect means:

   2. What does perfect look like?

   3. Is perfect really possible?

4. Who do you know who has a perfect life. Are you sure it is? If you looked deeper may you find more to the story?

5. Where can you take small risks, and take positive actions, even if they are not 100% perfect?

6. Look at helping others. Being in service, volunteering, or supporting others, especially those with similar problems to you, can be incredibly uplifting, energizing and take your focus off yourself and what you think may be wrong with you.

Worth is not best attached (or found) in external things like wealth, beauty, power and so on. Although some people attach a lot of significance to these qualities, if we give it some thought, we will realize that these are all temporary gifts that may not last. As high as we climb, we can also fall.

Intrinsic qualities, like kindness, loyalty, courage, empathy, compassion, and self-awareness are more lasting, and cannot be easily lost or taken away from us. Moreover, every living being has intrinsic worth and contributes in one way or the other to the world. It is not for anyone to elevate themselves higher or bring others lower. While humanity loves categories, labels, and having some sort of pecking order in society, there is a growing consciousness that worth is not connected to shallow, temporary qualities or the possession of resources. These things may be helpful in life, but they do not always define what is in our hearts and minds or the quality and experience of our lives.

MAINTAINING HEALTHY BOUNDARIES

All beings have intrinsic worth. What rights animals, the earth, or plants may have is open to interpretation. Life is random, and a lion eating a buck is not concerned with rights or boundaries, only with survival. Humankind has taken this to another level. We apply 'higher' thinking and rationalize why certain others should have or be less than us. Humans have basic rights written into law in many countries, although sadly there is still discrimination based on innate criteria like race, culture, gender, or religion. People look for reasons to be better than others, more worthy, and this is something we need to be aware of and challenge wherever we find such faulty thinking.

The first thing to keep in mind when thinking about your own boundaries is that you are allowed to say no to anything that is harmful or distasteful to you. This is a basic human right. If anyone has ever tried to convince you otherwise, they have had their own agenda in mind and not what is good or best for you at all. Crossing another's boundaries is bad on several levels. It can be abusive. It can be disrespectful. It can break down relationships, trust and disempower people. It can cause longer lasting psychological damage when someone's boundaries are consistently disrespected or ignored.

It's best to err on the side of caution when dealing with others, and respect certain universal boundaries like not causing others physical or emotional pain or taking what belongs to them, for example. What other universal boundaries can you think of? Are they universal or specific to you or your socio-cultural group?

Some of your personal boundaries are unique to you. They are related to your values and your needs. They help you know what is okay and what is not okay for you. This may be very different to how anyone else sees the world.For example, some people may be fine with a friend using their hairbrush or eating off their plate, while others may get highly offended by this behavior. Some hate swear words and others don't mind them. Some people like hugs and others hate being touched.

In a new relationship or meeting of any kind, if you have empathy, you will make an attempt to find out what is okay and not okay for your new social connections. You will not just assume this.

But so too there is a responsibility to share this with others. Boundaries need to be communicated or you cannot expect others to know what they are or always respect them. They might cross them accidentally, and unless you can communicate and maintain your boundaries, you cannot hold this against someone who is ignorant as to what they even are.

Before you can even communicate your boundaries, you need to get clear on what they actually are.

PRACTICAL EXERCISE: KNOWING AND MAINTAINING MY BOUNDARIES?

My Values	What is not okay for me (dislikes)?	Where are people crossing this boundary?	Have I communicated this boundary clearly?

Consider how you can share your boundaries:

1. First, be as direct and clear as you can, while still being kind and respectful. If you need to, restate the boundary. Sometimes people have fallen into certain habits and need reminding, but at some point you will need to draw a firmer line.

2. Where in your life do you need to start saying no? What is stopping you from doing so now? What would help you to do so? Consider starting with small 'nos' if you feel uncomfortable. Saying no can feel difficult at first. You could even practice saying it in the mirror or visualize the conversation going well.

3. You may expect a certain amount of resistance from people who have had things all their own way up until now. But this is where you need to make a decision as to whose life you are living—theirs or yours? If someone refuses to respect a boundary after you have respectfully communicated it, then maybe you need to look at avoiding them or taking some other more definitive action, as this is basically abusive behavior.

4. Practice not explaining why you are saying no. We often feel the need to explain and that weakens our point, especially with people who like to push boundaries. Make a list of different ways of saying no to common situations that you find yourself in and memorize them.

5. Get outside help if you need to. Keep records too. Bullies can be very skilled at ignoring others' wishes, and it may take some advanced skills to deal with their abusive behavior, if it can't be avoided altogether.

ATTACHMENT THEORY AND EXPECTATIONS

Being overly or unhealthily attached to something happening or being a certain way (an outcome), and subsequently investing emotions into that outcome, can lead to increased frustration or anger when that outcome doesn't materialize or happens differently to what we wanted. And, since a lot of life is outside our direct control (like what other people choose to do or say), we have basically handed over our power and our happiness to external events. This can lead to a roller coaster of feelings and a continual sense of being let down by life.

When we are disappointed it can feel pretty bad. In these cases, we have invested too much emotionally into something that could go any way, and are therefore likely to be upset in the end. By removing the emotions out of it, making plans, doing what is needful, but then stepping back and calmly letting the universe unfold, we stop that dreaded emotional roller coaster of worry and disappointment. It's just a more empowered, relaxed way to be.

Resisting what is—or the opposite, rejecting it and cutting all our emotions off about pretty much any of our hopes and dreams—isolates us and makes us angry and bitter. Detachment is reactive and also unhealthy for us. We need to feel our feelings, but we also need to decide how much of ourselves we will invest in day-to-day happenings so that we can maintain a calm equilibrium.

Emotional attachment to people is a slightly different affair. This is when you willingly choose to invest emotions in another being. But there is still a healthy way to do so, via unconditional love, or the way of frustration, when you get emotionally attached to what your loved ones do or say.

Unconditional love is the giving of kindness, care and love with no expectations of getting anything back, in any specific way. It is freely given, accepting and forgiving. It is not based on anything the other does for you in return. You simply love and want the happiness of the other. You are not in it for yourself. It feels secure as you have freely chosen to give this love regardless. It is similar to the love many mothers feel for an infant, or that a person feels towards a pet. It is easier to feel unconditional love for another being when you truly understand that you have no control over how they receive it or how it plays out. You simply give. If anything is returned that is a bonus, but you do not attach your emotions or ego to what or how that happens. This kind of love spans distance, time and all manner of pain that may have occurred because it does not rely on the recipient for its existence.

Unconditional love does not mean that you put yourself in harm's way or neglect your own needs consistently. You can feel love and still distance yourself from a toxic relationship, for example. You can feel love and still not agree with the another's choices.

Once we start dealing with other adults, however, we attach all kinds of conditions, ego-states, personal desires and expectations to them, and that makes the experience potentially destructive rather than truly loving. Conditional love limits, controls and weakens relationships. It makes people afraid of failure or making mistakes. It limits learning and growth.

Being mindful of how and what emotions you are attaching to outcomes helps you manage feelings better. This way your inner peace has a lot more to do with what is happening inside you than what is being done, externally, to you. If you are aware of unhealthy attachments and can step back and notice when you are too heavily or unhelpfully emotionally invested, then no matter how others behave, you will not be pulled into that emotional roller coaster.

This practice links into expectations too. Sometimes we have expectations that:

1. we have not communicated.

2. we have attached to in an emotionally unhelpful way. Then if we don't get what we want we get upset.

In these cases we can experience added frustration, dissatisfaction and anxiety while we wait for our expectations to be met. If we haven't shared and agreed on our expectations, though, all we can reasonably expect is for them to remain unmet.

PRACTICAL EXERCISE: CLOSING THE EXPECTATION GAP

Where in your life are expectations causing hardship for you? Where are you using the word 'should' for other people's actions and getting angry when they don't do what you want?

If an agreement around what you want versus what they want is not possible, what else is possible? Perhaps a compromise or an exchange might work better in this particular instance? Have all of the possibilities been reasonably explored and is this exchange really vital to your relationship and well-being?

List what you are expecting. Where are you frustrated or feel your needs are not being met?	Have you communicated your expectations and did the other person agree?	Is this reasonable? Does every person you know do this? Might there be another way?

WATCHING YOUR WORDS

The words you use every day about yourself, how you feel, what you are worth, or any other aspect of yourself, become true and real through repetition.

Your subconscious mind is always on, always listening and recording. It stands to reason that if you start saying something unhelpful, negative or destructive over and over again, this recording will become pretty loud. It will replay whenever you are faced with a similar challenge, or any challenge for that matter. It will take away your confidence, and ensure that you only focus on your weaknesses which will appear insurmountable. Anxiety soon follows when your words are always 'I can't'.

Other phrases people tend to use when engaging in negative and self-deprecating talk are:

1. This is too much for me.
2. This is too hard.
3. This is a nightmare.
4. It's impossible.
5. No one/everyone/I always/I never... [insert negative words here].
6. I'm not ready/unable/drowning/ crushed/overwhelmed.
7. I'll try... (rather than 'I will').
8. Why me?
9. I am [insert bad feeling or label].

I am sure you can add some words to this list. Sometimes our words become our approach to life, and are based on the root belief that we are not good enough. Sometimes they are labels we, or others, have given us. These labels limit us. They reject the notion of any other possibilities or choices.

For example, you may have failed at a few things, but that does not make you a failure in everything. You may have a terrible habit of impatience, but that does not mean you can't improve. Labelling yourself a failure, or impatient, limits the chance that you might change or improve. You make whatever happens next a horrible foregone conclusion, when it does not need to be.

Using emotive, hard words t0 describe situations or yourself so frequently will eventually trigger bad feelings. This will make whatever it is you need to do next that much harder, because those negative emotions make it hard to focus or stay motivated.

As you already know from your study of this book, your words are based on thoughts, which trigger various chemical reactions in the body. Bad feelings follow negative thoughts, and then worse choices, like avoidance of problems, depression, anxiety, substance abuse and various other psychoses, follow as well.

You are quite literally being your own worst enemy instead of your best friend. If you were to hear a stranger say these same things to someone you cared about, your instinct would be to step in and stop the abuse. And yet, we feel no qualms about saying such harsh things to and about ourselves. You need to remind yourself that you should be your own biggest supporter. You need to build yourself up, not break yourself down. If you can't do it, how can anyone else?

PRACTICAL EXERCISE: WATCHING WORDS

What are the go-to words that break you down rather than building you up?

My negative word habits (Things I say a lot about myself or challenges)	How could I say this better, differently, or in a more positive, supportive way?

You need to stay mindful of the words you use. Choose active, more supportive and clearer words that commit you to your chosen path. Drop the hesitation, self-deprecation, fear-based language, and anything that makes you feel less-than.

When anything challenging arises, or you are suddenly in the middle of a big feeling, use a both passive voice and a curious voice to describe it to yourself.

Previous Unhelpful Words	Calming and Objective Words
I am... [insert negative label]	Sometimes I [label], but I am getting better at [desired action/state].
I will try.	I will do it.
I am feeling [x].	I notice I am feeling [x]. I wonder what this means?
This situation is...[insert negative label].	How fascinating/This is not great right now, but I'm going to be okay.

Over time you will become better at this, and your new, more positive language will help move, inspire and motivate you and others.

CHAPTER 6:
HOLISTIC HELPERS

You are getting better at wielding and using the tool of the mind. You understand the body-brain connection and what thoughts and feelings have to do with overall anxiety. To add to the arsenal of things you can use when life gets a little challenging, here are a few tips and tricks I have learned along the way and that will function as extra building blocks to help you remain resilient.

WORKING WITH ALL LEVELS OF THE MIND

We have spoken previously about our subconscious mind. In a nutshell, the subconscious is that part of your mind that is not in your focus as conscious thought in a given moment. It is a reservoir of all that you are, recorded and kept for the time that you might need to retrieve a bit of data from the past that relates to your situation in the present.

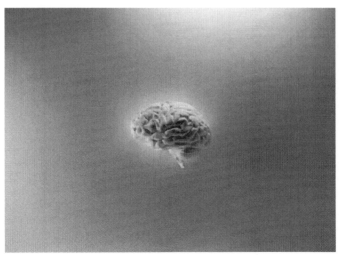

It is more than simply memory. It is active and recording, filtering and categorizing as you go about your day. Repeated words or actions are given extra space and energy, whether this is what we are doing or what is being done by others around us. Each thing you act on creates less opposition to similar, successive actions. That is what underlies habit formation.

We also now know that our subconscious prefers to process images, emotions and sensory input over abstract concepts. It does not judge, only records. And most importantly for our purposes here, we know that the subconscious does not distinguish between what is real and what is not. This is why when you watch a scary movie, even though you know logically you are in no danger, you still get scared. That's your subconscious at work, and it is very literal. Imagination is thus way more powerful than knowledge.

Time is not relevant. For our subconscious there is no past or future, only now.

Finally, it does not process negatives that well. If you say "I will not eat after 8pm at night," it just deletes the 'not'. It hears and focuses on "eat after 8pm", and this makes it more likely that you will do so. It also cannot hold opposing ideas that well. Once an idea has been accepted by your subconscious, it stays until it is replaced by another idea.

Your conscious mind forms a gateway between the world and your subconscious. You consciously decide what to do, say and so on. You consciously decide what you will or won't believe. If something, like a positive affirmation for example, does not correlate with what is already in your subconscious mind, your conscious mind will likely reject it. So simply telling yourself you are rich, beautiful and so on is not enough, if that goes against previous programming.

However, once something has crept into our subconscious, via repetition, strong emotion or when the gatekeeper is distracted, it is pretty hard to dislodge. In fact the more you consciously try to force your subconscious to think a certain way, the less effect you will have on it. You must instead take all this information and get a little clever in your management of your mind.

It's a bit like convincing a toddler to eat their broccoli. A direct, frontal assault will only end in tears and tantrums. You need to sneak the broccoli in in disguise, chop it up small and hide it in the bolognaise sauce, or present it in such a way that it is fun and appealing.

Knowing all of this, we can formulate a slightly different plan to shift unhelpful programs out and replace them with more useful ones.

VISUALIZATIONS

So you know you get anxious in certain situations. Or perhaps there is something you want to achieve that you feel less than confident about right now. This is a great time to access the power of your subconscious mind. Using powerful imagery and emotions, we can communicate what it is we want. Since the subconscious does not know the difference between real and unreal, if we can walk ourselves through a well-constructed visualization often enough, it will be for our minds as if that thing has already happened several times in reality, successfully. Thus, when you actually do or say the thing in real-life, it will feel familiar, and you will have a deep, inner confidence that boosts chances of actual success.

Knowing how this works means we need to do so in a very specific way, however.

PRACTICAL EXERCISE: VISION INTO REALITY

Pick one goal at a time; we don't want to confuse the issue with too many instructions all at once. Choose a situation that often triggers you or where you normally feel anxious. Alternatively, choose a situation that you want to be true in your life, that right now is a bit of a struggle for you. Play it out as you would like it to be.

1. Get very clear about what it is that you want to happen. Be specific around what, how, when, with who, where and so on.

   For example: I would like to enjoy social events with friends, like parties, and outings.

   Be careful not to use any negatives or visualize outcomes you don't want. That just focuses your mind on exactly what you are trying to change and reinforces the old stuff you are trying to replace. Always flip it into the positive. So if you don't want to feel anxious around strangers, rather say "I feel relaxed talking to new people".

2. Have a dash of realism added. If you know that losing weight is a problem for you, saying "I will lose 20kgs by next Tuesday" is going to stretch the disbelief of the strongest mind. Rather, stating something that is more possible and believable, like "Every week I am losing weight" is more acceptable to the mind, and can be tweaked and made into a bigger goal once the first idea is accepted.

   With our example above, we could say: I am relaxing more around other people and feel fine talking to friends and strangers.

3. Picture it as if it was a movie playing out before your eyes.

4. Now write this wish in the present tense and include the strongest emotions you can with it. Add in any sensory details that might help you see, taste, touch, smell and feel this wish as it would be in real-life. This becomes your visualization script.

5. For example: I enjoy parties and outings and feel relaxed, accepted and enjoy this social time talking to all kinds of people and making friends.

6. Either record the script you have written onto your phone for playback during meditation or write it into a few short sentences and add images off the internet, out of magazines, or hand-drawn. If you put it onto paper or card, in this way, it becomes a vision board, in essence. Make sure to use keywords and keep it present tense, and add in all the good emotions you feel (or will feel, but as if it's happening now). Stick that up wherever you will see it a lot, like by your work area or on the washroom door.

7. The best time to access your subconscious with your visualizations is when you are very relaxed, like right before bed or on waking or while meditating. Having visuals around you also starts working on your subconscious mind slowly, as

you see the vision board a lot and that starts filtering in over time.

I have used this mind trick so many times for both myself and my clients. It works when you approach it in the manner described above, and there is no set amount of times or set duration needed. Just visualize often enough that the vision starts feeling natural for you. Then take it on the road, and test it out in manageable real-life situations. Start small: Perhaps a few words to a stranger at a party at first, or just being at the event, and slowly build towards the overall behavior goal.

Be patient and kind with yourself, and let go of any harsh, negative criticisms. Any actions and words that move you closer to your goal, even if just a little bit, are a win.

AFFIRMATIONS

Just like visualizations, affirmations need to be:

1. focused on what you want (and not what you don't want)

2. written in the present tense, as if they are happening now and happen often

3. attached to a positive emotion

4. specific and detailed enough to meet your end goal. Just like making three wishes, our mind can be a bit tricky and sometimes give us exactly what we asked for, but not what we really wanted. Spend some time focusing on all the details of what it is you want.

5. Write out your affirmations and repeat them out loud right before bed and on waking. Print them out and stick them up. Engage with them as much as possible.

Again, there is no specific timeframe, but in my experience affirmations done in this way come into being and become a new reality within a few weeks. This is not law of attraction stuff, as along with your affirmations you will also need to keep your focus on changing your actual behaviors too. Just saying you want more friends, but then never going out your front door or creating a situation where people can engage with you, is not enough. The idea behind visualizations and affirmations is that they empower you and give you the confidence to attempt your ideas in real-life. They reduce the anxiety around trying out new things as your mind believes you have tried it and it has worked before. If it worked before, successfully, the odds are that it will work again, and that there is no need to feel anxious since you are dealing with what feels familiar to you.

Some affirmations I have used, or helped others create include:

I am loving the freedom of being self-employed.

I have time to enjoy self care.

I am earning enough to be comfortable and meet all my family's needs.

I am working with amazing clients who give me great feedback and reviews.

I feel safe and calm.

No matter what happens, I choose to respond calmly.

These are all future "wants" written in the present tense, with emotions included. For more ideas look online for affirmation examples, as there are many great ones listed already to choose from and alter to suit your needs.

PERSONAL MANTRAS

An extension of the above tool is the calming and affirming personal mantra. This is simply a short sentence that you use when feeling anxious. It is intended to be calming and empowering. It becomes almost like a protection spell that you can weave around yourself when you are feeling especially triggered or stressed out.

It's best to choose words that have meaning for you, and they don't have to be complicated. For example:

1. Let it be.

2. Let it go.

3. I'm okay.

4. How fascinating.

5. I'm safe.

6. Right now, at this moment, I'm alright.

7. This feeling will pass.

8. This situation is temporary.

9. I will make it through this.

10. I can do this.

Whatever your mantra, make it your best friend. Keep coming back to it, learn it and use it often.

If you find yourself in a moment of intense anxiety, other than using movement to help lessen the adrenaline in your system, you can also recite your mantra over and over again, quietly or just in your own head, while focusing on your breath. Sitting quietly, slowing your breathing, and reciting your mantra for a few minutes can take you from hyper alert to a more manageable state.

Another way to use personal mantras to calm anxiety is to have a personal tune or song that embodies the calm feeling that you want. Play it as often as you need to when feeling anxious to help you calm down.

Be on the lookout for any negative self-talk or other people who tend to say unhelpful things to you repeatedly. Reframe your self-talk and avoid anyone who breaks you down, criticizes you continually, or otherwise makes you feel consistently less than them or disempowered. Remember that repetition strengthens the thought, so if you have someone repeatedly filling your head with unhelpful ideas, you are letting them program your subconscious in ways that do not serve you. You sometimes need to fight for your own inner peace and take a long-term view of how certain input is not helping you at all.

THE BUDDY SYSTEM

Have a go-to person who understands and supports you without complicating your life with their own agenda. This is generally someone kind, calm and compassionate who has experienced anxiety themselves and hopefully understands enough about it to be a proper support for you.

There may be anxiety support groups in your area, and perhaps someone who has struggled with anxiety and overcome it themselves (from within the group) may feel empowered to help you out as needed. Perhaps you could be mutually supportive of each other.

You need to agree on the parameters and expectations on both sides and make sure that everyone is clear and committed to the agreement. What is okay and not okay? What time and energy can be offered on both sides, and what you can each do for the other? Sometimes a person is happy to just be there if you need to talk or to help you get through a specific event or challenge.

While it may feel like a big ask, many people actually would feel honored to help you out. It does not have to be forever, but it can help either one of you over a rough patch. Maybe there is something you can do in return, or perhaps you just deepen an existing friendship by reaching out and connecting vulnerably and authentically. Maybe down the line you can be this person for someone else who is struggling, and pay it forward in this way.

A buddy can:

1. Travel or do outings with you, if you are worried that anxiety or panic attacks may happen when you are out and about. They would need to know what to do or say in the event of you losing your cool and not get too phased by it.

2. Provide a neutral, listening ear when you need to vent, express emotions or talk something through.

3. Remind you of the basics, as well as all the stuff we have covered in this workbook. Share this book with them if you feel it will help. Often when you are in the middle of a hard

time, you forget the simplest resources, and a gentle reminder to use self-care and other anxiety tools is all you need.

4. Keep an eye on you, and check in if they know you are having a particularly hard time.

While we may feel that our friends should automatically fulfil these roles, it is a fact that everyone has their own problems, responsibilities and paths to walk. While it is great if someone comes forward and just naturally fills this role, you cannot expect it. There is just simply too much going on for most of us. We are there in a limited capacity, but then need to focus back on our own lives, families and challenges.

Remember the story about unhealthy emotional attachment to expectations, especially ones we haven't communicated or agreed on with others? That approach to relationships only leads to frustration and disappointment. However, if you set aside some time to verbalize your anxiety, and literally ask for the help you need in the specific way that you need it, you are much more likely to receive it.

NATURE AS A HEALER

Getting away from the noise, hustle and bustle of urban areas, and finding a cool, green spot to unwind and ground yourself is a great way to relax.

Just the noises and events of a normal day spent around many people can stress you out on a number of levels. The sound of a siren, a drive to the office or the requests of family and coworkers can leave you feeling drained, stressed or overwhelmed, especially when it all starts adding up.

Even if you live in the heart of a busy city, you can still find a small piece of nature and make it a daily part of your self-care.

Consider any one of these examples:

1. A trip to the local park, or any natural area nearby, like a beach, greenbelt, or your own back garden

2. Creating a green spot on a windowsill, with potted plants, rocks and other natural items. You can sit in or near it and still feel a connection to nature on some level.

3. Looking up at the stars, or watching the clouds float past

4. Sitting in the sunshine

5. Meditating with a plant or tree as your focus

6. Walking your dog (and yourself) somewhere more natural, even if it is a slightly more green road nearby with a few trees

7. Visiting a local fresh food market or farm

8. Taking a weekend or day trip to your nearest natural area or nature conservation spot. Pack a backpack, take a good friend and make an adventure out of it!

Any time spent outdoors has been shown to lower blood pressure, muscle tension and heart rate. It engages your parasympathetic nervous system which is all about rest and relaxation. This naturally reduces anxiety.

Urban greening, and even 'green' rooms fitted out to simulate forests, mountains or beaches, are increasingly being made available in big cities to help reduce the stress, mental distress and related issues that come with living in large, condensed groups of people. In Japan they call this *shinrin-yoku* or forest-bathing. Studies are rolling in with data to support using nature as a healer In one study, they compared people walking for 40 minutes in the lab versus an actual forest and the results showed a direct reduction in the stress-chemical cortisol among the forest walkers (Sifferlin, 2016).

Get into nature in whatever way you can. Take off your shoes and sink your feet in the grass or sand. Feel the breeze on your face and the sun warming you. Smell the fresh air, breathe deeply of it. Listen to the sounds of nature: bird calls, wind shushing and beetles clicking and whirring. Really immerse yourself in the moment.

When I am unable to connect in any way with nature, then I resort to water as my one connection. Getting into water, in a bath, shower or pool, is one of my favorite ways to calm my body and mind.

Nature grounds excess energy. It slows us down and reminds us that there is more to life than just our problems. Mother Earth and all her bounty can hold and support us, just as she always has.

THERAPY

Sometimes we need a little added help. Finding a therapist that you can connect with and who can support you through trying times is no different than going to a doctor when you have a cold. You need to look after your body and your mind.

There is less stigma these days related to seeking external, professional support. Just having the chance to talk a situation through with a neutral, objective person can help release a lot of pent-up anxiety.

There are also many options these days: art therapy, nature therapy, talk therapy, support groups led by professionals, life coaching and more.

Another type of therapy is exposure therapy, where you are very slowly, in a controlled and safe way, exposed to the source of your fears. I find visualization exercises useful for this if the thought of real-life exposure is too stressful. It is always best to let a professional guide you through a desensitization process like this.

Although you can work through a lot on your own, if you feel in over your head then consider letting a trained professional support you for a while.

With anxiety can come depression, obsessive-compulsive behaviors, suicidal thoughts and panic attacks. These are serious, and can have significant repercussions if not treated from all angles. If you are suffering from a range of symptoms over and above mild anxiety, you may need temporary help in the form of therapy and perhaps even medication. See this as a stepping stone to your health on all levels. You can continue to work on yourself, using this workbook, alongside many other therapies.

CONCLUSION

® ® ® ® ® ® ® ® ® ® ® ® ® ®

My vision for this process is one led by you, that can be customized to wherever you are in your life right now.

Our modern world is chockablock full of potential stressors, from supervising your kid's homework, to planning the next family holiday, paying the bills , driving to and from work, chores, shopping, responsibilities, and all kinds of conflicts that come with being around other people.

A well-known psychologist, Susan Davids, has a fabulous quote I love sharing with regards to this:

> I've had hundreds of people tell me what they don't want to feel. They say things like, "I don't want to try because I don't want to feel disappointed" or, "I just want this feeling to go away."
>
> "I understand," I say to them, "but you have dead people's goals. Only dead people never get stressed, never get broken hearts, never experience the disappointment that comes with failure. Tough emotions are part of our contract with life. You don't get to have a meaningful career or raise a family or leave the world a better place without stress and discomfort. Discomfort is the price of admission to a meaningful life."

We cannot have a life free from challenges, but how we learn to process, manage and cope with them is what will decide whether we have a mostly calm, enjoyable life or a less pleasant one mastered by our thoughts and feelings.

We need to be the master of the ship. We need to understand how our bodies and brains work in tandem and how to process unhelpful thoughts, or alter poor self-care, so that we don't feel bad all the time.

It starts with acceptance of what is. We have many expectations of life. The traffic should be faster, people should be more polite, this job shouldn't be so hard, my partner should be more attentive, my teenager should behave. We attach our emotions to these outcomes when we have little to no control over how these things actually play out.

But how is that working for you? Do these things magically improve because we are angry or upset? How much time and energy do we waste? How many stomach ulcers do we get as a result? Let go of attaching emotions to outcomes and notions like, "I will be happy when", "It must work this way or I will be upset" type of thinking. That way lies disaster, unnecessary frustration and anxiety. Drop the 'shoulds'; rather get used to saying, "It is this way, now what?"

Only when we let go of our resistance (and emotional reaction) to what is happening can we see the situation more clearly and deal with it effectively. Mistakes, rejection, disappointment and all kinds of challenges are inevitable. Sure, you can plan and manage things to some degree, but you can't always prevent whatever change is coming.

What you can do is strengthen your mental, physical and emotional resilience, so that no matter what happens you are able to adapt and keep going. Not to mention that a life without challenges and change is a life without learning and growth. Yes, many things can be learned through love, in a calm way, but many significant life changes only come after some sort of breakdown and mental or lifestyle breakthrough and shift. We need to experience some hard stuff, from time to time, to help us shift and grow.

Since life can be challenging, mental and emotional hygiene needs to become a daily lifestyle and be practiced often. It needs to be learned, used and taught to our children as a matter of course. Just like we learn to put a plaster on a wound and brush our teeth, we also need to learn how to deal with our hearts and heads. The fake, false positivity of the last few decades is toxic. Pretending to be always strong, always fine, when inside we are crumbling, is not helpful. Once we understand that most of us feel challenged from time to time and acknowledge that we also feel this way, we open ourselves up to support and understanding we might not have gotten otherwise. Being open and vulnerable is brave and shows strength of character, not weakness or irrationality. Just alter your openness to the situation. Too many of us have learned to shut ourselves down, pretend we are fine, and avoid the hard questions and self-care we need. We numb ourselves with alcohol, or other substances, or distractions, and then don't understand why our lives feel so out of control and messy.

If we don't acknowledge and allow our feelings, how can we know what it is they are telling us? How can we know what we need to do next, to stay resilient and support this vital part of who we are?

You know the story of the pink elephant right? You're not thinking about one right now are you? Did you? I bet you did! This little exercise tells us that trying not to think about a thing or feel a feeling does not work so well. Trying to avoid and suppress our anxiety, and its triggers, will not work.

Telling yourself, "I will not be upset, I will not be angry/sad/mad/crazy" does not work either. In fact, it just encourages you to focus on the thing you don't want. More thoughts about the problem bubble up and your mind goes down the rabbit hole.

Unmanaged thoughts, negative self-talk, and the quality of our thoughts in general will lead to our experience of life. Thoughts lead to feelings which lead to actions. We need to notice and name our feelings, sit with them, and see what these feelings are trying to tell us. In that way we become a scientist of ourself.

Are we anxious? What happened right before that? What were we thinking? Can we change that thought or situation? Or maybe we just need a meal and a nap, and when we wake up we will feel better automatically, because that was the real issue? Or perhaps we need to channel our feelings into some sort of productive activity, and work off a few of our excess stress chemicals?

When we become the driver not the passenger of our mind, we decide to stop letting unconscious thoughts, unhelpful mental meanderings or distracted thinking control our lives. Becoming mindful and practicing being in the moment and fully present helps strengthen our control over where our focus goes. Your mind and feelings go where your thoughts go, so you have to learn to steer your thoughts where you want them to be.

Listening to others who have travelled your path of overcoming anxiety and sharing stories also helps you gain much-needed perspective. We are all different, but we'll also share some universal human experiences. Everybody has it hard in some way, everybody! As a counsellor, I hear so many stories and each person feels that their situation is real and challenging for them, or they would not be seeking help. This is not a competition either. We want less pain and suffering in the world. We want more self management, self awareness, healing and happiness because that makes us nicer, better people, and that has a knock-on effect on everyone and everything around us.

Look over your fence and see that other people's yards are also in a mess. Everybody copes differently, and most people's bad behavior is about them and their unresolved issues. Getting curious, rather than reacting, to others' bad behavior helps you take a step back and not take everything so personally.

Consider using what you have learned to be of service to others. Helping others strengthens us and also helps us internalize and consolidate our own learning. Lastly, find your joy! What energizes and excites you? You need to do more of that, whatever it is. Purpose and meaning bring that all-elusive happiness and joy we all want, and more besides. Having a meaningful life, full of uplifting and supportive connections to others and meaningful relationships, is what has been shown time and again to be the key to joy, satisfaction and inner peace.

For those days when it is particularly tough don't lose sight of the many tips, methods and exercises shared with you here. Go back to them as often as you need to and use them again and again. It is no good complaining that you feel anxious all the time, and yet also staying stuck in inactivity around the issue. Fear can freeze you, for sure, but it does not freeze you all the time, and even if you start small, with little lifestyle tweaks, and engage with the bigger stuff when you feel stronger, you will still start noticing a difference in your anxiety levels as a result.

There is no one solution to our mental and emotional wellbeing, but many. You choose which ones to use, when and how. Whatever you do needs to work for you. So pick and choose from amongst the chapters and exercises, and go with what feels right, right now. There is no specific order you need to do any of this in. To reduce anxiety we need less to-dos, musts and complexity.

Even though I have been counselling people for many years, I still have moments when I don't feel great. I've gotten through a rough relationship, as well as many other life challenges, and so the talk I talk is also the walk I walk. Many of these exercises I go back to over and over myself because each time there is new insight and learning for me. Each time the practice makes me just a little bit stronger and more resilient.

When times get tough, and my mind starts messing with me, the difference now is that I know what to do with that. I know the signs my body and feelings are sending my way and what they mean. I know how to process feelings and use them like a sniffer dog to unearth root problems in my life.

Helping others uplifts me, too, and when I'm not doing that I'm enjoying a good book, practicing my piano skills, and enjoying family time with my three kids and husband. My life is mostly peaceful and anxiety free. Once upon a time that wasn't the case. Once upon a time I was a mess, and then I started healing. In those dark moments, it felt like there was no end in sight to the pain, but now, looking back I wish I could tell myself, "Hey, you've got this!"

I can't travel back in time, nor am I sure I would want to, as all those experiences led me here, to this place where this workbook has become possible. Remembering what I went through has made writing this for you so incredibly important to me.

I hope that it has added as much value to you as this work has done for me. In the end, there is no need to live a painful, unhappy life when a much better one is just a few steps away. If any of my words have helped you, please feel free to share your experiences with readers in a brief review. Your feedback is important to me and will help other readers decide whether to read the book to.

I wish you, the reader, all the strength and peace you desire.

Thank You!

Shirley R Lynn .

REFERENCES

10 most common physical symptoms of anxiety. (n.d.). Intrepid mental wellness, PLLC. https://www.intrepidmentalhealth.com/blog/10-most-common-physical-symptoms-of-anxiety

Alvarez, Domingo. (n.d.). [Love emoji]. Unsplash. https://unsplash.com/photos/Cs3y8Mn6-Gk

Barcelo, Carl. (n.d.). [A woman doing a yoga pose]. Unsplash. https://unsplash.com/photos/nqUHQkuVj3c

Bloom, Estudio. (n.d.). [Doing my best]. Unsplash. https://unsplash.com/photos/KvkvaFlZdSg

Clode, David. (n.d.). [Fighting baboons]. Unsplash. https://unsplash.com/photos/Cjdcpj4l2NM

Do you have brain inflammation? How to know and what to do. (2012, June 25). The Functional Neurology Center. https://thefnc.com/research/do-you-have-brain-inflammation/#:~:text=What%20causes%20brain%20inflammation

Fakurian Design. (n.d.). [A rendering of the brain]. Unsplash. https://unsplash.com/photos/58Z17lnVS4U

Fears we are born with. (n.d.). https://thriveglobal.com/stories/fears-we-are-born-with/.

Fleming, Sean. (2019, January 14). *This is the world's biggest mental health problem - and you might not have heard of it.* World Economic Forum. https://www.weforum.org/agenda/2019/01/this-is-the-worlds-biggest-mental-health-problem/

Gatewood, Hal. (n.d.). [A ball of energy with electricity beaming all over the place]. Unsplash. https://unsplash.com/photos/OgvqXGL7XO4

Grenar, Gianfranco. (n.d.). [A sad, depressed man, sitting alone in the darkness]. Unsplash. https://unsplash.com/photos/eTNtXTEB2Jg

Heftiba, Toa. (n.d.) [Jewish Memorial Berlin - human reconnection between love and hate]. Unsplash. https://unsplash.com/photos/_UIVmIBB3JU

How does trauma affect the brain? - And what it means for you. (n.d.). Whole Wellness Therapy. https://www.wholewellnesstherapy.com/post/trauma-and-the-brain#:~:text=It%20perceives%20things%20that%20trigger

Fuuu, J. (n.d.). [A woman on a beach with arms out looking at the sun]. Unsplash. https://unsplash.com/photos/r2nJPbEYuSQ

Kahveci, Mert. (n.d.). [A man who has fallen asleep on the couch while reading]. Unsplash. https://unsplash.com/photos/Rfnljr9AlDk

Loftus. (2019, October). *Speaking of Psychology: How Memory Can Be Manipulated.* www.apa.org/research/action/speaking-of-psychology/memory-manipulated.

Manfredsteger, Pixabay. (n.d.). *Mindmap* [Photograph]. Pixabay. cdn.pixabay.com/photo/2018/09/26/09/13/pixel-cells-3704048_960_720.png.

Molliver, Julie. (n.d.). [Tools]. Unsplash. https://unsplash.com/photos/Z3vFp7szCAY

Nascimento, Bruno. (n.d.). [A person wearing bright orange running shoes on a set of stairs]. Unsplash. https://unsplash.com/photos/PHIgYUGQPvU

Netz, Yael. (2017). Is the comparison between exercise and pharmacologic treatment of depression in the clinical practice guideline of the American College of Physicians evidence-Based? *Frontiers in Pharmacology, 8*(257). https://doi.org/10.3389/fphar.2017.00257

Olson, David E. (2021). The Promise of Psychedelic Science. *ACS Pharmacology & Translational Science.* https://doi.org/10.1021/acsptsci.1c00071

Openclipart Ventures. (n.d.). [Boomm]. Pixabay. https://pixabay.com/vectors/explosion-detonation-blast-burst-147909/

Polekhina, Diana. (n.d.). [The man seals the wound with adhesive plaster]. Unsplash. https://unsplash.com/photos/rKJoUsqmSs4

Robertson, Kate. (2021, May 26). *Psychedelic Therapy: Uses, How It's Done, Risks, and More*. Healthline. https://healthline.com/health/mental-health/psychedelic-therapy

Robson, David. (2011). *A brief history of the brain*. New Scientist. https://www.newscientist.com/article/mg21128311-800-a-brief-history-of-the-brain/

Shaw, Callum. (n.d.). [A woman drinking a cup of tea at a window]. Unsplash. https://unsplash.com/photos/i1zD8-hp9xg

Sifferlin, Alexandra. (2016, July 14). *The Healing Power of Nature*. Time. https://time.com/4405827/the-healing-power-of-nature/

Swancar, Adrian. (n.d.). [A man holding his face in pain]. Unsplash. https://unsplash.com/photos/_2NHZjSMLjA

Tran, Anthony. (n.d.). [A woman sitting on a black chair in front of a window]. Unsplash. https://unsplash.com/photos/vXymirxr5ac

Unrau, Sebastian (n.d.). [A forest]. Unsplash. https://unsplash.com/photos/sp-p7uuT0tw

Vang, Nong (n.d.). [Pennywise the dancing clown]. Unsplash. https://unsplash.com/photos/5EOAoPiq56U

Walton, Alice G. (n.d.). *7 ways meditation can actually change the brain*. Forbes. https://www.forbes.com/sites/alicegwalton/2015/02/09/7-ways-meditation-can-actually-change-the-brain/?sh=1b32a1414658

Why Are You Anxious? (n.d.). https://www.youtube.com/watch?v=iALfvFpcItE&ab_channel=AsapSCIENCE

Winter, Isabell (n.d.). [A man meditating on the roof of a building in front of a skyline]. Unsplash. https://unsplash.com/photos/lzYZEDJ8fbo

Yousaf, Usman (2020, November 1). [Frustrated Young Man Screaming in Fear]. Unsplash. https://unsplash.com/photos/8dvyPDYa35Q

Made in the USA
Columbia, SC
18 August 2023

21819802R00061